From Yellow to Golden

Malcolm Morecroft

Herkimer Publishing™

Published by Herkimer Publishing™ in 2014
www.herkimerpublishing.com

This book is dedicated to
Anne and Frank Weeks

For their assistance in writing this book and for sharing
the information that they have gained over many years.

❧ Acknowledgements ❧

I am more than grateful to Sharon Lynn and Lorenzo Guescini for their advice and assistance with regard to this book and for the design work and lay out.

I would like to thank the friends and families of the relatives of the people included in this book who have willingly supplied me with photos and information to be included. This includes Anne Cowe, Helen Frost, Jessie Harrow, Lynn Kipps, Jenny Stirling, Fiona Thurm, Clare Singleton, Chris Pawson, Angharard Meredith, Constantia Nicolaides, Julie Yealand, David Cork, Sir John Lister-Kaye, Peter Mills and George Purvis. My thanks to the many Archives around the country all of whom have so willingly supplied me with documents and photos, some of which have taken many hours of searching through boxes and photo albums hidden away for many years.

My special thanks to Elizabeth Anne Jolley, for encouraging me to write this book and for her valuable comments.

My grateful thanks to Mary Jarrett for giving me advice with regard to the presentation and publishing of this book

Thanks also to Alistair Smith at Turriff, Aberdeenshire who supplied the Tweedmouth Tweed.

My sincere thanks to my beloved wife, who during a period of ill health while I was writing this book looked after me with great care and consideration.

~ Contents ~

❦ From Yellow to Golden ❦

Introduction

T HIS BOOK FOCUSES on a small group of people, who over a period of seventy years developed a breed of dog, originally known as the Yellow Retriever, which by the early 1900's was known as the Golden Retriever.

It looks at the family history of these people and shows how, despite their varying positions in society, they came to work together and their lives intertwined to make the breed so successful as a working dog and in the show ring. They were all devoted to the breed and in their individual ways ensured that they developed into one of the most popular breeds of dog in the 21st century.

The seven people that I have written about have all left a lasting legacy. This legacy is enjoyed everyday by owners of this breed.

Dudley Coutts Marjoribanks

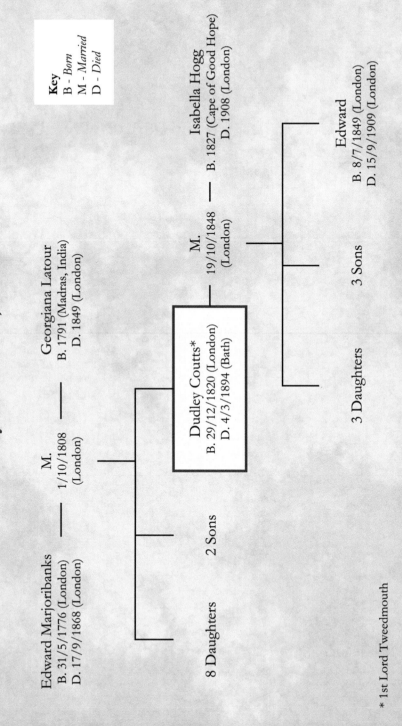

Key
B - *Born*
M - *Married*
D - *Died*

Edward Marjoribanks
B. 31/5/1776 (London)
D. 17/9/1868 (London)

M.
1/10/1808
(London)

Georgiana Latour
B. 1791 (Madras, India)
D. 1849 (London)

Dudley Coutts*
B. 29/12/1820 (London)
D. 4/3/1894 (Bath)

M.
19/10/1848
(London)

Isabella Hogg
B. 1827 (Cape of Good Hope)
D. 1908 (London)

8 Daughters

2 Sons

3 Daughters

3 Sons

Edward
B. 8/7/1849 (London)
D. 15/9/1909 (London)

* 1st Lord Tweedmouth

❦ 1 ❦

Dudley Coutts Marjoribanks

(29th December 1820 - 4th March 1894)

Setting the Scene

T HE SURNAME MARJORIBANKS can be traced back over 500 years. Like most surnames of this long duration they often denote an occupation or have a reference to land holding. The nearest one can get to either of those with this surname is to the latter, with Debrett's of 1831 suggesting that the name derives from a part of a dowry of land from King Robert 1st, given to a Marjorie Bruce on her marriage to Walter Stewart in 1315. These lands were claimed to be in Dumfriesshire but the exact location has never been determined for certain and there are no references to this surname in this part of Scotland in the 14th century. Although there are a number of people who had this surname in Scotland at the start of the 20th century, there would appear to be hardly any who are associated with working the land. There does, however, seem to be agreement as to the pronunciation of the name as being phonetically - Marchbanks.

By the early 1700's the major concentration of people with this surname were in the central belt of Scotland. At this time, the area around Edinburgh was expanding rapidly and a number of the

Marjoribankses were to play their part, being involved in various commercial activities. Among those involved was an Edward Marjoribanks, born in 1738, who had an interest in banking. He became good friends with Thomas Coutts who had set up his own private bank, which supported many of the tradesmen and merchants at this time. Edward married Grizel Stewart in 1761 and they had five sons, the fourth of which, another Edward, was born in 1776. Through his father's friendship with Thomas Coutts, the son Edward went to work at the bank. Thomas was quick to recognise the same sound business principles by which he wanted in the running of the bank and in 1798 he made Edward a partner, a post that he held until his death in 1868.

Under the leadership of Thomas Coutts the bank quickly established a reputation for prudent and sound judgement in financial matters. By the middle of the 18th century the bank had opened a branch in London with Thomas and his brother Patrick overseeing the business.

Thomas Coutts lived in a frugal manner and he often looked shabby in his appearance. He took delight in relating that, on a visit to Brighton, a benevolent person took pity on him and gave him a guinea. It was never spent but has found a good home, in the archives of the headquarters of Coutts Bank in The Strand, London. Thomas was not interested in the luxury trappings of a person in his position. He found pleasure in living in very modest conditions in a property in St. Martins Lane, within walking distance of The Strand, and it was to this property in May 1763 that he brought his bride - and his marriage caused quite a stir. Instead of someone in high society he married the daughter of a Lancashire farmer by the name of Susannah Starkie. She had come to London as a housemaid and found work with James Coutts, another brother of Thomas. The marriage brought a sudden change in the life of Susannah. From being paid £8 a year she was now married to one of the wealthiest men in London but she fitted in well with Thomas's lifestyle. He more than likely knew that she valued living life modestly but comfortably. During the next 12 years they had seven children, 4 boys and 3 girls. Sadly the 4 sons did not survive. The three daughters, Susan, Frances and Sophia did, and all had an excellent education. The marriage lasted for over 50 years, towards the end of which Susannah was suffering from dementia and quite violent mental attacks. Her death came suddenly after she scalded herself with boiling water and she died on the 11th January 1815.

Thomas remarried three days after the funeral of Susannah, this time to an actress by the name of Harriot Melon although his surviving children did not know of this second wedding for several weeks. Thomas had first set eyes on Harriot at the Drury Lane Theatre, which he often visited in the year before the death of his first wife. She maintained that Harriot Melon was her real name but her birth, parents and upbringing are a mystery. After the marriage Thomas continued to live at the same property in London but Harriot had bought a small villa in Highgate and would travel to London in her own carriage. She maintained that she financed all of this from her appearances on stage. If this second marriage was to be a shock to his surviving children another was to come. After 7 years of what had been wedded bliss, Thomas died on the 22nd February 1822, and when the contents of the will was made known, he left all of his estate to Harriot for "her sole use and benefit". One can only surmise the consternation with which his daughters received this news, despite the fact that by this time they had all married wealthy husbands, Susan to the Earl of Guilford, Frances to the Marquess of Bute and Sophia to Sir Francis Burdett. However, although the husbands had grand titles, they may have been expecting a windfall on the death of Thomas Coutts. If that were the case then the consternation would have been even greater!

By contrast Edward Marjoribanks, born in 1776, chose a lifestyle that befitted someone that had been appointed as a partner to a leading bank of the time. Edward moved to London in 1805. On the 1st October 1808 he married Georgiana Latour at St Mary, Marylebone, London and they went to live at a sizable property at 34 Wimpole Street, London. Georgiana was born in 1791 in Madras India. She was the third child of Col. Francis Latour and his wife Ann. The family home was Hexton House in Hertfordshire. On the 19th July 1810, Georgiana gave birth to her first child, a son who was named Coutts. By the time of the 1831 census they had a sizable family of 2 sons and 8 daughters. Sadly, by this time their eldest son, Coutts, had died on the 2nd April 1829. The others sons were Edward born on 15th June 1814, and Dudley Coutts on the 29th December 1820. The census also lists 18 servants, who no doubt were kept busy with such a large household.

Of these children, it is their third son, Dudley Coutts Marjoribanks, that the dog world and the lovers of today's breed of Golden Retrievers, owes so much. It is thanks to him that with his interest in shooting, outdoor sports and crossbreeding of dogs that we now have the intelligent, loving and affectionate breed that is so popular today.

Dudley was baptised on the 19th January 1821 - accompanied by his elder sister Harriot! - born a year before but baptised on the same occasion. Tutors who visited the home in Wimpole Street

Photo 1: Edward Marjoribanks
(partner at Coutts Bank)

were responsible for the children's early education. In September 1833 Dudley was sent to Public School at Harrow and placed under the teaching of the Rev. Charles Thomas Longley, at this time also the Head Master of the school. Dudley was at Harrow until 1836 but a year before this he started to keep a "stud book" listing the dogs kept by his father at his country estate. This is not laid out as a stud book of today. It is very much a list of dogs, and on many individual entries it has the name of the sire i.e the dog, and dam i.e the bitch for the dogs in the ownership of his father and in the future what Dudley owned. Compared with a modern stud book it is more of a stock take, taken at the end of each year. For most years the lists also include the number and type of game shot at the close of the shooting season and the estate which he was shooting over. After Dudley bought his own estate in Scotland, he added some notes about the keepers that he employed and there were comments about the weather for that year, which in some years had a significant effect on the number of game bagged. These lists have survived and in the mid 1960's Dudley's granddaughter, the late Lady Marjorie Pentland placed them in the safe keeping of the Kennel Club. The value of these lists for an historian cannot be underestimated.

Why did Dudley start the list in the first place? It is probably safe to assume that it was from his father Edward, who in 1831 purchased Stanmore Park in Middlesex. This was 11 miles from London, a relatively short distance from his home in Wimpole Street. The grounds extended to over 1,000 acres consisting of extensive grazing land and 300 acres of woodland. The house, on two floors, had 23 bedrooms, drawing and dining rooms and various rooms for guests to be entertained. There were also a large number of servant's quarters. The grazing land was ideal for Edward for his outdoor

Photo 2: Dudley Coutts Marjoribanks
(1st Lord Tweedmouth)

pastime of breeding Polled cattle. Edward would have needed to keep records of his cattle for breeding purposes. It is more than likely that he gave Dudley the task of listing the dogs on the estate. For the first year, 1835, he lists 2 Setters - Carlo and Don, 4 Greyhounds - Muta, Ruby, Rosette and Lolsby, and 4 Spaniels - Comet, Jet, Bounce and Tan. He also gives details of where they were bought from or who gave them. This also gives some interesting information. One of the Greyhounds, Muta, was given by Sir Edmund Antrobus, also a partner at Coutts bank, and another, Lolsby had come from Dudley's uncle, Col. Latour from Hexton House. Another interesting note at the bottom of the list, and one which he kept through the years, was the "head of game" and for that year it is put down as - "Stanmore Park, head of game, 238". In future years this part of the list would become more detailed but it was not until 1852 that the list of dogs would include retrievers. Dudley continued to use Stanmore Park for his annual shooting until 1840 when he shot at Easton Neston, Northamptonshire, the estate of Lord Pomfret. He must have been goods friends of the Marjoribanks family, as on the 1841 census Dudley's sisters Harriot and Julia are staying at Neston House. Dudley continued to use these grounds for shooting until 1846 and the following year he and Lord Pomfret rented Upper Killin in Perthshire. This was the first time that Dudley had shot north of the border and he must have been well pleased to record 3,108 grouse bagged.

After Dudley left Harrow he went to Christ Church, Oxford, to read law and on the 23rd January 1845 he was admitted to the Middle Temple, London. On the 28th January 1848 he was called to the Bar. Later that year while Dudley was riding through Hyde Park he set eyes on a beautiful young lady, by the name of Isabella

Hogg. Three weeks later he made an appointment with her parents, the Rt. Hon. Sir James Weir Hogg and his wife Mary Claudine nee Swinton. He asked them for permission to marry Isabella. This was agreed, and three months later on the 19th October 1848 the marriage took place at St George, Hanover Square, London. Despite what could be classed as a near society wedding at a foremost church in London, reports of the marriage are brief with no indication as to who attended the ceremony or the reception, which was held at the bride's parent's property in Berkeley Square. From here Dudley and Isabella went to Porters Park, Shenley, in Hertfordshire for their honeymoon. There may have been another reason why they wanted what appears to be a low-key wedding - and no she was not expecting at this time! A more likely explanation could be that neither of them liked publicity and Dudley, especially in his younger life did not court the limelight and very few pictures of him or Isabella have been found. However, on the stud book for 1848 he put down - "Fawley Court, head of game 342" - and then in bold writing and in part underlined, he put "Married 19th Oct". One would hope that Isabella was pleased with this acknowledgement of their union!

On the 8th July 1849 the first child, a son, Edward, was born. The following year they had a daughter, Mary Georgiana, and then in 1852 another son Stewart born 23rd July. At this time they were living at No 4, Upper Grosvenor Street, in the fashionable Park Lane area of London. By this time Dudley appears to have forgone his barristers work - the 1851 census gives his occupation, "Barrister, not in practice", but he had been appointed as magistrate for Middlesex and for Inverness-shire. He also became a partner in the brewers Meux and Company. Dudley kept his interest in the sporting field and from 1848 to 1850 he again used Fawley Court in

Buckinghamshire for the shooting season. The following year Dudley returned to Scotland renting Guisachan in Strathglass, Inverness-shire from Captain William Fraser of Culbockie for £420. His list for the 1851 shooting season, records the head of game as 972, considerably down on the previous year at Fawley Court. He returned to the same estate the following year and then in 1853 he rented the Novar estate in Ross-shire.

By the early 1850's he decided to go into politics and in 1853 he stood for Parliament as a Liberal candidate for Berwick on Tweed and was returned with a substantial majority. His increasing love of Scotland and its shooting opportunities were made manifest in 1854 when he purchased the Guisachan estate of some 20,000 acres. Guisachan in Gaelic means "Place of the Firs" and the estate had these in abundance. In the spring and summer there was a profusion of wild flowers. When it rained, it rained! The surrounding hills and mountains provided a myriad of streams and waterfalls, the largest of which is the Plodda Falls. The water rushing off the high ground added to the very special attraction of the area that survives to this day.

It has been reported that he got Guisachan for a knock down price of £53,000 but the previous owner Captain Fraser did not have the finances that were needed to modify the estate. It had the potential to be one of the foremost shooting grounds for game of all types, north of the border. Dudley had the finances and over the next few years he spent large amounts of money to make improvements for what was to prove to be the benefit of all those who lived and worked on the estate. Within the next few years he completely modified the main house and added a conservatory to the west side. He employed Wright and Mansfield, the leading London firm of

Photo 3: Guisachan - "Place of the Firs"

designers at that time, to design the interior decorations in the Adam style. Stables were also built, one being for the working horses the other for horses that were made available to guests visiting the estate. Other buildings were erected to look after the well being of his pure-bred cattle - and within these there were Highland and Aberdeen Angus lines and in keeping with his father's interests there were also Polled cattle, these being bred from pure pedigree stock. On the surrounding estate new cottages were built, a school was opened, a laundry and brew house provided.

Not all of the residents in the area at this time agreed with all these changes despite the fact that Dudley was doing his utmost to improve their living conditions. The crofters and farmers were given the option of new leases and a better way of life, which some did not accept and chose to move away but none of them were forced out. Giving evidence at the Crofters Commission held in Kingussie in 1883 he gave full details of the changes that he had made which were of benefit to the residents. By the time that he gave evidence to the commission the changes were complete, his model village, now named Tomich, was there for all to see.

The other very important buildings that were built were - The Kennels! These were built at the side of an existing cottage, a few hundred yards away from the main house, the dwelling being modified for the use of the kennel men and Stalkers. The floors to the runs of the kennels were paved in glazed terracotta tiles, making it easy to hose down and keep clean. Inside they were centrally heated, with a large boiler used to heat the water in the pipes running on both sides of the kennels. The heating system was also used for cooking and preparing the food for the dogs. Separate pipes ensured that there was always a fresh supply of water that was fed into cast-iron drinking bowls and the structural design was done in such a way as to eliminate draughts but also to provide a fresh flow of air. Whichever breed was housed in the kennels the dogs lived in excellent conditions and were looked after extremely well. After a hard working day they deserved to be pampered during their time of rest.

During the early 1850's Dudley's stud books become of more interest. In 1852 the first Retrievers are listed, although in rather an odd format. Midway in the list of Pointers he put down, "Gypsy, Retriever sire Col, dam Steam, pupped June 1850." A note is then added below which stated, "The above Pointers and Retrievers with William Tomline at Guisachan also Robert Dixon". It has not been possible to confirm who William and Robert were and in addition to this what type of retriever Gypsy was. By this time Dudley had stopped listing a colour for his dogs, so again no help there. Gypsy was not listed in the stud book for 1853 or 1854 - still with William Tomline and Robert Dixon? - but she is listed as Gyp in 1855 and it must be the same dog as on both the lists for 1852 and 1855 it states that she was pupped in June 1850. The list for 1858 confirms she was a bitch, as two puppies, by Paddy, called Alma and Kass, were pupped in January 1857. It is somewhat odd that they do not appear on the list of the year before - perhaps they were again with William Tomline or Robert Dixon, something we will never know. For the details of this dog we have to look again at the list for 1855, where it is recorded "Paddy, bought at Brighton, November 1854, pupped 1854." No description is given of the type of retriever, or a name for the puppies that would have given an indication of their colour. In the list for 1859 only Alma is recorded but in the following year another mating had occurred with a pup, Garry, being recorded. These two dogs continued to be listed for the next three years, then in 1863 they are joined by Tweed, with the additional detail "Ladykirk bred, pupped 1862". The name and the short description give valuable information. Ladykirk is a large house on the River Tweed and at this time David Robertson, Dudley's cousin, occupied it. Although Tweed was listed under retrievers it is almost certain that this was a Tweed Water Spaniel, a breed of dog that is now extinct.

To date it has not been possible to obtain an authenticated picture of this type of dog but at this point I must give my thanks to Anne and Frank Weeks, for all the research and time they have spent trying to find a picture over many years and who have readily shared this information with me. So it was with some very good luck that while my wife and I were on holiday in the Borders of Scotland in 2013 that we were able to get somewhere near to what we have all been trying to find. The first piece of luck was at the Eyemouth Fishing Museum, where I was given the name of George Purvis who had worked on the Tweed all his life and that I could make contact with him from the grounds of Paxton House, seven miles upstream from the mouth of the Tweed. On a perfect early summer's day I met George and one of my first questions to him was "Do you know of the Tweed Water Spaniel?". His immediate answer was "Yes, big dog, web feet". I then asked about the colour. Without hesitation he replied "Liver". The answers from George were very much in line with what was already known but the confirmation by someone who had known of the breed was even more important when he also told me that a woman who lived in Coldstream, further up river on the Tweed, had one in the 1950's. Although George had never seen this dog he did know the breed and it did give a far later date of it still being in the canine world than had previously been known. Following my meeting with George, I then contacted the archivist at Paxton House who let me see the private photo albums of the grounds and the people who lived there and visited in the late 1800's and early 1900's. Amongst them was a picture of a dog called Ponto. His likeness had striking similarities to that given in Richard Lawrence's book, *The Complete Farrier and the British Sportsman*, published in 1816. He describes the dog as large but not too heavy with long hair, naturally curled, eyes prominent and lively, a short thick neck, broad shoulders, pastern joints strong and forefeet long and round and dew clawed. He also gives the information on the colour of the dogs - "black, the best and hardiest, spotted or pied, the quickest of scent, and the liver colour the most rapid swimmer". Add all these attributes together and they make an ideal mix to crossbreed, to obtain a thorough working dog for all terrain. Richard Lawrence also adds that he had seen these dogs working along the Tweed and the shoreline of Berwick. Another person who would probably have seen this type of dog was Thomas Bewick (1753-1828), the famous natural history author and engraver, who included in his work a water dog, which has striking similarities to Ponto. Dudley, through his cousin David, would have had every chance to see these dogs at work and decided to try a crossbreeding. He already had experience from his father on what to do to improve the rearing of his dogs and although he may have had some doubts of the outcome he must have been fairly certain of what the results would be.

Dudley may have wanted to use Tweed in crossbreeding but the last time this dog is on the stud list is 1866 when he would have been 4 years old. At this young age one can only assume that he had had an accident or that he had succumbed to distemper, which in those

Photo 4 (Left): Illustration of a Water Spaniel c.1803
Photo 5 (Right): Ponto (by permission of Paxton House Trust)

days was fairly prevalent. Dudley must have seen a positive side to the working ability of this breed, as in 1868 another dog from David Robertson is listed by the name of Belle, again with the added information, "Ladykirk bred". This is also the year when the Brighton connection is once again recorded, with a dog by the name of Nous listed and the additional information "Lord Chichester bred". Although Brighton is mentioned again, the listing of Paddy in 1855 does not have any reference to whose breed it was. The question with Nous is, what was this dog's background?

It is well recorded that one Sunday, Dudley was walking with his son Edward on the downs above Brighton - yes Brighton again! - and met a man, a Shoemaker by trade, who had with him a light coloured retriever. He told them that he had acquired the dog in return for a debt owed to him from Obediah Miles, a Gamekeeper who worked on the Stanmer Estate north of Brighton that was owned by Lord Chichester. Dudley very much admired this dog and he offered the Shoemaker a sum of money to buy the dog. The Shoemaker must have thought more of the money than the dog as he accepted his offer but only on condition that being a Sunday the sale would have to wait until the next day. When the purchase was completed Nous was sent to Guisachan. This information was given by Dudley's great-nephew, the 6th Earl of Ilchester, and passed down by him to Dudley's son, Edward. I have no doubt that this information is largely correct but where does Obediah come into it? - where did he get the dog? - why was it noted on the stud list as "Lord Chichester bred"? I have not been able to get any indication as to what dogs Lord Chichester or his Gamekeepers had on his estate or if he had any interest in breeding dogs. It must certainly have been a retriever and I believe it was a flat coat, but not a black flat coat. The one picture that we have of Nous shows a light coloured dog - light, yellow? - and it is not impossible that a dog with a black coat could have produced some light coloured pups in a litter. The eminent biologist, Professor Thomas Huxley (1825-1895) stated that yellow is the primary colour of almost all wild dogs and if yellow puppies are kept from a litter out of black dogs the resulting bitch puppies from a later mating will almost certainly produce yellow puppies, even if they are crossed with a black dog. There are also other accounts from the Scottish Field, Country Life, Our Dogs and The Times, all giving various reports of how Dudley came to have Nous and again it concerns Brighton. The accounts relate that when a touring circus visited this town in the 1850's he saw, possibly with his son, Edward, a "troupe" of dogs performing various tricks on stage. Dudley was so taken by these dogs, their looks and their nature that he bought all of them and sent them to Guisachan. There are several flaws with this account. Firstly the word "troupe" covers not one in number but could be

Photo 6: Nous (dog on the left with rabbit in mouth) with
a group of Gamekeepers in front of Guisachan House

up to eight, but at no time on the stud book that Dudley kept, are there more than six retrievers listed. In no one year is there a large influx of retrievers from any one place. Seeing what Dudley had put down on the lists (i.e. Ladykirk bred, Lord Chichester bred) I believe that he would have made a special note of this purchase. As it is, Nous appears on the list as a single dog purchased at Brighton. In fairness to the earlier reports at the time that were written, there would have been no access to lists that Dudley kept.

Although Dudley did not have the opportunity to use Tweed for crossbreeding, he did use Belle and in June 1868 a litter by Nous is listed with two puppies by the name of Primrose and Cowslip. But there had been a third puppy, as Crocus is listed in 1870 with the additional note - "Edward's". This puppy must have been with his son Edward the previous year, when it was not listed, but in 1870 Edward was in America hence the reason why it appeared only on the list for 1870 and 1871. Crocus must have been returned to Edward when he came back to this country, as he is not recorded on the lists after 1871. Without Dudley noting the colour of the three puppies from Nous and Belle, by calling them Primrose, Cowslip and Crocus it is evident that they were all yellow.

In addition to Dudley's time spent modifying the house and estate at Guisachan, his duties in Parliament also had to be attended to. His immediate family was also increasing, although this was tinged with sadness. His second daughter, Annie Grizell was born in October 1855. She was baptised at the Chapel Royal, Brighton on the 1st November 1855 but died on the 20th August 1856. A third daughter, Ishbel Maria was born on 14th March 1857. Two other sons were to complete his family, Coutts born 6th December 1860 and Archibald born 25th November 1861. Sadness came to the family again in 1864 when the second son, Stewart, died suddenly on 22nd January after contracting scarlet fever.

His life in public also presented him with problems. Parliament was in turmoil during the late 1850s. In 1857 Dudley was returned as MP for Berwick on Tweed but another general election followed in 1859, when he was defeated. However, within weeks the elected MP stood down and in the resulting by-election he was returned as MP. He successfully defended his seat in 1865. A year later he was made a Baronet. When the general election was called in 1868, he decided not to stand. It is not known why he made this decision but in this year he knew that his father's life was drawing to a close. For a long time he had expected to take the place of his father as a partner at Coutts bank but unbeknown to him the decision had already been made not to appoint him. This in part was down to the grand daughter of Thomas Coutts, the philanthropist, Angela Burdett Coutts. She respected the wishes of her grandfather who did not want the Coutts family outnumbered by the Marjoribanks family in the running of the bank. Added to this was Angela's opinion that Dudley had not been "trained in business habits". On being informed that he would not be made a partner, Dudley flew into a rage and lost his temper, much to his disadvantage, but it was to prove to Angela, among others, that they had made the correct decision, as his actions were not in line with the way that the bank should be run. At Coutts, quiet courtesy was the rule. A last plea to his father to act on his behalf came too late. His father died on 17th September 1868, aged 94. He had been a partner for 70 years. There is no evidence that his elder brother Edward wanted Dudley to take the place of their father as a partner as he appears to have remained silent on this issue during this time. Dudley was not altogether the loser in this, as when the will was read, the bulk of his father's wealth was left to him and although his brother was left far less in the will, Dudley obviously did not hold a grudge against him, as in 1878 he saved Edward from bankruptcy after he incurred debts of over £200,000, mainly due to the building of a new house in Bushey Park, Hertfordshire.

These events and reports of him "flying into a rage" and "losing his temper" have often been cited with regard to his character, even at times hinting that he was of a dangerous nature. This opinion ignores all the favourable reports of him. Even before the money that was left to him by his father he was a very wealthy man and his wealth increased substantially when, through his friendship with the brewer Sir Henry Meux, he was appointed a Director of Sir Henry's company. From the outset he took an active interest in the running of the company, ensuring that the business progressed steadily and that it created healthy profits year on year. In the running of the company he was known as being firm but fair and always ready to consider the views of others and to put their views into action when it was of benefit to the company. Away from his business activities his modernisation of the estate at Guisachan had provided the people working there with first class amenities. There is also a most touching tribute in the stud book list for 1873 to his Head Gamekeeper. It reads "Simon Munro who lived with me as keeper and dog breaker since 1856 died on the 1st November, aged 44, an attached and faithful servant, kind hearted and warmly interested in his employers and their sport - I miss him much and his loss will be sorely felt, DCM".

These are positive attributes to his character that should be known. The evidence of the kindness and consideration to those around him are far greater than reports of his irascible temper.

Dudley continued to develop the breeding of his "Special Yellow Retrievers" but there was no great change in the number of these dogs in his stud books. In 1870 there are 5 and in 1879 there are only 4. In this period there are some notes of interest. Firstly, on the 1872 list another dog by the name of Tweed - pupped the same year - is listed again, given by David Robertson. This dog was used in a mating with Cowslip a year later. Secondly, in 1874 Dudley records " Brass, Lord Ilchesters, Ada sister to Crocus and Cowslip pupped May 1874". This confirms that Lord Ilchester had been given a bitch by Dudley, the only bitch up to this time that he had given to anyone and he must have given his permission for Lord Ilchester to breed from this dog. Brass did not appear in the lists after 1874 as it was given into the care of Duncan MacLennan. Brass became a great favourite of Duncan and his family. Then in 1876, a Labrador! by the name of Crony, is listed with the note "given to J Carnegie by Miss Hagart". What did Dudley's "Special Yellow Retrievers" think of this? Not much by the looks of it - it did not appear in the list for the following year or ever again! Then in 1877 Dudley lists Jack and Gill that had been born in 1875 out of Cowslip with the sire being "Edward's Red Setter, Sampson". So it appears that Dudley and his son tried a cross breeding, possibly to improve the colour of the breeding line. Also in this year and distinctly headed "puppies" there is a record of Minos and Zoe born in March 1877 with the dam being Topsy - out of Tweed and Cowslip - and the sire being "Henry Meux's Sambo". Surely the latter must have been black or brown. So despite the fact that there was no great change in numbers during this time there were some other dogs coming into the breeding line although with the exception of Henry Meux's dog these are from close family connections. Was Dudley experimenting again in the breeding line as he had done with Belle and Tweed? I believe it could have been more than likely as it was less than 20 years since Nous, the first of the yellow retrievers, had come to Guisachan and Dudley would have wanted to continually improve the breed which he treasured so much.

The number of dogs listed during this time may not have changed a great deal but the "head of game" showed a huge increase, proving that all of the work done on the shooting parts of the estate was paying dividends. On average over 2,500 different types of game birds and stags were recorded as bagged in the shooting season and the visitors book for this time gives an insight to those that were invited to join Dudley and the family for the annual gathering. Among them were William Vernon Harcourt MP - whose son was to play his part in the development of the breed in later years - Sir Henry Meux, his fellow director at the brewery and the same person who brought Sambo to Guisachan. The 5th Earl of Ilchester, Henry Edward Fox-Strangeways, Dudley's nephew, and Dudley's uncle, Col. Latour were also regular guests. Then there were those who were to become related to the Marjoribanks family of the future. The Duke of Marlborough came with his three beautiful daughters, one of which was to capture the heart of Dudley's son Edward. There was Lord and Lady Aberdeen whose son was to marry Dudley's daughter, Ishbel, and there were members of the White Ridley family whose son was captivated by Mary Georgiana, Dudley's eldest daughter. They were to marry on the 10th December 1873. Also on the guest list on more than one occasion were the Archbishop of Canterbury - for the shooting, the beer or to say grace? - and Mr Gladstone the Prime Minster. The first guests would arrive in early August and stayed for up to three weeks with the season coming to an end towards the end of October. It was no doubt a very busy time for all those that worked at the house and on the estate.

Photo 7: Brook House c.1870

On the 1871 census Dudley and his wife were living at 29, Upper Brook Street, a property they had acquired in 1856, with Mary now 20, Ishbel 14, Coutts 10 and Archibald 9. There were also 18 members of staff - six of whom came from Scotland. No one was living next door - but the builders were hard at work. Dudley had bought number 28 the previous year and he again employed Wright and Mansfield to design the interiors to make the two properties into one. By doing this Dudley was able to extend the gardens, which were a favoured play area for the children and their friends who came to visit and he retained the brook, which ran through these gardens and hence the new name for the property of Brook House.

One of the most admired features of the completed property was the ballroom which could hold over 200 guests and Dudley had an ideal chance to show this off when his eldest son Edward married

Fanny Octavia Louisa Spencer-Churchill on the 9th June 1873. The marriage took place at St.George Hanover Square, London, with the reception at Brook House where the wedding gifts were displayed in the new ballroom.

A year later, Dudley and Isabella became grandparents with the birth of a boy on the 2nd March 1874 who was christened Dudley Churchill. Two other children of Dudley and Isabella were married in the 1870's. In 1873 their eldest daughter Mary Georgiana was married on the 10th December to Matthew White Ridley, MP for North Northumberland and eldest son of Sir Matthew White Ridley of Blagdon, Northumberland. In 1877 their third daughter Ishbel Maria was married to John Hamilton Campbell Gordon, son of the Earl of Aberdeen on the 7th November. Ishbel must have been dearly loved. By getting married in November, Dudley missed a part of the shooting season at Guisachan! All of these sons and daughters had married sons and daughters of guests at the annual Guisachan gatherings for the shooting season.

There was also sadness during these years. His cousin, David Robertson, who shared Dudley's love of dogs with his Tweed Water Spaniels, was elevated to the peerage three days after Dudley's son Edward had married and he took the title Lord Marjoribanks. Seven days later on the 19th June 1873 he was knocked down and killed by a horse-drawn bus outside his club in Newcastle. With the sons of David Robertson predeceasing him, the title became extinct. Within 10 days the pleasure that the family had had in the wedding of Edward must have faded quickly when they received this news. It has often been recorded that the peerage given to David Robertson was the shortest on record but this is not so. This dubious accolade goes to artist, Sir Frederick Leighton, who took the title Baron Leighton on the 24th January 1896. He died from a heart attack the following day. It's difficult to beat this!

The grand weddings and the expense incurred for three of his children during the 1870's did not stop Dudley acquiring more property. In 1876 he bought the Edington Estate in Berwickshire, which included Hutton Hall, from John Maclean Mackenzie Grieve. The Hall, overlooking the River Whiteadder, a tributary of the Tweed, is three miles from Chirnside and in Dudley's parliamentary constituency. He set about making modifications - by now he had plenty of experience - and when he had finished he renamed the property, Hutton Castle. Another attraction of this property was the 12000 acres of moorland with plenty of shooting potential, and plenty of work for the "Special Yellow Retrievers".

In 1881 Dudley was elevated to the peerage and took the title Baron Tweedmouth of Edington. In recognition of this Dudley was presented with a valuable oil painting of Berwick-upon-Tweed, given by his constituents in recognition for all the hard work that he had done in representing them throughout 25 years in Parliament. His work on their behalf continued until the late 1880's although he changed his allegiance from the Liberal party in 1885 and joined the Unionist party. Dudley was kept busy with his business activities during the 1880's added to which he had to resort to the courts to sort out more than one problem. In 1883 Sir Henry Meux died. Dudley had supported his fellow Director and shooting enthusiast through a long court case, which called into question Henry's sanity. This was with regard to a codicil that he added to his will and which his family challenged. The court found in favour of Sir Henry. Following his death his only son, Sir Henry Bruce Meux, took Dudley to court, claiming full control of the brewery. Once again the court ruled in favour of Dudley. On his Guisachan estate there were problems with him having to resort to the courts north of the border. In 1883 he had given some of the grazing rights in Glen Affric over to a Mr Winans. He was an American millionaire and he quickly started to fence the land. This was all well and good with the exception that the fences were also erected across the roads on which the tenants of Dudley relied for their daily work. On more than one occasion the fences were broken down only to be re-erected within hours. Mr Winans must have badly judged the Scottish Highlanders who did not take kindly to their work being hindered, added to which they were also loyal to Dudley and his family. Matters came to head in 1885 when Mr Winans was passing through the village of Tomich and stones were thrown at his carriage. A reward of £500 was offered for the capture of those responsible. The tenants remained true to Dudley. The reward was never claimed! The matter ended in the courts with the revelation of some heated letters between both parties giving their differing views of the situation. Mr Winans did not like what he regarded as private letters being aired in public. He certainly did not like the verdict, which was given in favour of Dudley.

The stud book that Dudley had kept during the 1880's continues to be of interest, despite the fact that his handwriting, which was never the clearest, becomes somewhat more indistinct. As with the lists for the 1870's there are a number of family links with the dogs being bred. The highest number of retrievers listed in any one year during this time is 7. Listed in 1881 is Sweep, "bred by Lord Ilchester, Crocus bred", and he also notes it is with McDonald, one of his Gamekeepers. Sweep was a year old at this time and was used in a mating with Zoe, the resulting litter having at least three puppies named Sol, Jumbo and Saffron. In 1882 the retrievers listed are

Topsy, Zoe, Minor, Sweep - still with McDonald - Sol, Saffron and Jumbo. In 1883, Topsy, and Sweep are not listed but a note is given that "Zoe and Jack - Edwards" - had been sent to Duns Castle - at this time rented by Edward - and had a litter of 3 Yellow pups on the 5th March 1884! Dudley confirms this litter on the list for 1884 but gives 4 yellow puppies, Nous - the second dog to have this name - Tansy, Gill and Guinea although this last entry also has the note "by Sweep out of Zoe March 1883". The 1885 list also has an addition dated 1886 when Tansy was destroyed for chasing the sheep at Guisachan but the list also has Minos, Nous, Jumbo, Saffron and Gill recorded. The last two of these are with W Macdonald and Hugh Fraser respectively. Another entry in 1885 lists a retriever named Bobbie out of Moonstone and Guinea "given by F Graham and bred at Netherby". There is a tentative connection with Dudley for this entry as Sir Frederick Graham had his shooting estate at Netherby, Cumberland and at a shooting party held there on the 18th November 1884 Dudley's uncle, Sir John Marjoribanks died suddenly. Bobbie is listed again in 1886 but does not appear in the following year, although Moonstone does, as its brother, Zelstone had been mated with Edward's Gill the resulting litter producing 10 puppies, all black. Not all of these puppies were kept on the estate but in 1889 one of these, named Quennie, had been mated to Nous - the second - and from this litter two puppies, Prim and Rose, are listed. These two names do indicate that these puppies were yellow whereas those either given or born in the 1870's and 1880's and named Sambo, Sweep and Zelstone must have been black or brown. When Dudley first started his stud book in 1835 he recorded the colour of the Pointers, Greyhounds and Spaniels. By the time the first Retrievers were listed he had stopped making a note of the colour of the dogs, in fact the column headed colour had now been changed to - remarks. Well - the latter were of great interest but - Dudley, it would have been good to have the colour as well!! Despite this - very many thanks for keeping these lists for so many years!

The last year of Dudley's was 1890. On the list there are 10 pointers, 4 deerhounds and 5 of his "Special Yellow Retrievers". The names for these are given as Jumbo, Charley, Nous, Gill and Saffron. There is no mention of any game shot in this year. By 1890 Dudley's health was deteriorating and he had heart problems. He still spent time at Guisachan but his visits were becoming shorter. When he visited the estate in July 1893 he made arrangements for the sale of his entire herd of pedigree cattle. This took place at Beauly Station, on the Highland Railway line, the place being chosen so that buyers could quickly transport their purchases to new grazing lands. All the cattle were sold in one day with some record prices being paid. The tenants at Guisachan must have been saddened to see the cattle being driven the twenty miles from Guisachan to Beauly Station, never to return. It was during this visit that his daughter Ishbel, now Lady Aberdeen came to visit with her husband prior to them going to Canada, where he had been made governor general. It was to be the last time that she saw her father.

Dudley and his wife remained at Guisachan until the start of 1894. Many of his tenants remarked that the bracing air of the north had been good for his health. They returned to their London home on the 10th January1894. Within weeks Dudley again fell ill and in the first week of March they went to their property at Prior Park, Bath which they had purchased some years earlier. Dudley's physician Dr Douglas Kerr, also accompanied them on the journey and at first the change appeared to be of benefit to him but on the afternoon of the 4th he suffered a heart attack and died shortly after 4.00pm.

When the news of his death reached Guisachan the tenants were deeply shocked. Although they knew that his health had not been good for some time, the realisation that the person who had had such an effect on their lives for over 40 years had passed away, was received with great sadness. In Berwickshire, where he had served his constituents over many years as their Member of Parliament the news came with equal sadness. In both these areas of Scotland he had been respected by people in all walks of life and done his very best for them. His legacy lives on. He provided us with one of the most beautiful, gentle and popular breeds of dog in the canine world. Or should this be "THE" most beautiful, gentle and popular breed of dog in the canine world?

Dudley's body was returned to his London home on the following day. Two days later his funeral service took place at Quebec Chapel at the Kensal Green Cemetery. The list of mourners contained many family members and some that had been regular visitors at Guisachan for the shooting season. Among the former was his wife Isabella, now the Dowager Lady Tweedmouth, his son Edward now Lord Tweedmouth, and his wife Fanny, now Lady Tweedmouth. His nephew, Haddo, represented Dudley's daughter, Lady Aberdeen who was in Canada. His son-in-law, Sir Matthew White Ridley, also attended. Among the many friends who had enjoyed the shooting season at Guisachan over the years were the Duke of Roxburghe, Lord Randolph Churchill, Lord Balfour, Lord Ilchester, Lord Curzon and Mr F Leveson-Gower.

After the service his body was interred in the family vault, which had been erected by Dudley and his father in April 1859. The first members of the family to be placed in the vault were obviously brought from a previous resting place. His mother, Georgiana, who died in 1849, his uncle James, who died in 1867, his brother, Coutts, who died in 1829, his sister Annie Caroline, who died in 1833, a still born child who was not baptised and of which no details have been found. His son, Stewart who died in 1864, his father, Edward, who died in 1868 and recorded in error on the cemetery records as Edwin, and Maria, his sister, who died in 1882. Two years after Dudley was interred his unmarried sister Emma was laid to rest. Dudley's nephew, the Hon.Archibald died in 1900, Dudley's wife the Dowager Lady Isabella Marjoribanks died in 1908, Dudley's sister Julia Madelina, the widow of William Malet Dancey died in 1910, and Dudley's unmarried sister Laura who died in 1920 were also interred in the family vault. In total fourteen family members occupy the vault and having visited it I can confirm there is room for more. Although I can also confirm that there is little chance of anyone else being added!

Dudley's will was made public on the 14th April 1894. He left a personal estate of £714,861 6s 4d. This equates to over £42 million today. The bulk of his estate was left to his son Edward. He made sizable amounts available to his widow, Isabella. Smaller amounts were left to his daughters, Mary and Ishbel. Seven others in the family were also left money and his sons Coutts and Archibald were each left half of the shares in Meux brewery. The domestic staff that worked at Brook House at the time of his death were left money of varying amounts, in accordance to their length of service and on a similar basis over 20 employers at Guisachan were left money. The highest amount of £150 was paid to Duncan MacLennan - nearly £8,000 in today's money - no doubt as a genuine thanks for all the care that he had given to his dogs and his "Special Yellow Retrievers".

The family vault is situated on the North side of the cemetery, now hemmed in by roads that are seldom quiet. Further North - over 600 miles in fact - can still be found the remains of the mansion that Dudley built, now roofless and looking rather forlorn. The peacefulness of the area remains as it was in Dudley's days, with its abundance of fir trees and the streams and rivulets still tumbling down from the mountains and hillsides where Dudley enjoyed his days throughout the shooting season. On the day that he was laid to rest his "Special Yellow Retrievers" were still at work and would remain so for many days and years to come.

Edward Marjoribanks

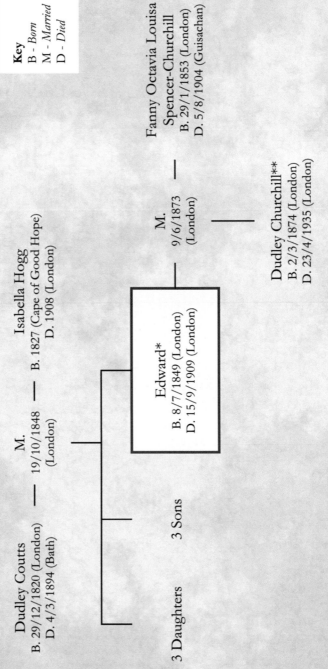

Key
B - *Born*
M - *Married*
D - *Died*

Dudley Coutts
B. 29/12/1820 (London)
D. 4/3/1894 (Bath)

M.
19/10/1848
(London)

Isabella Hogg
B. 1827 (Cape of Good Hope)
D. 1908 (London)

Fanny Octavia Louisa
Spencer-Churchill
B. 29/1/1853 (London)
D. 5/8/1904 (Guisachan)

M.
9/6/1873
(London)

Edward*
B. 8/7/1849 (London)
D. 15/9/1909 (London)

Dudley Churchill**
B. 2/3/1874 (London)
D. 23/4/1935 (London)

3 Sons

3 Daughters

* 2nd Lord Tweedmouth
** 3rd Lord Tweedmouth (No male heir)

❧ 2 ❧

Edward Marjoribanks

(8th July 1849 - 15th September 1909)

Following in Father's Footsteps

AFTER DUDLEY COUTTS MARJORIBANKS died it was left to his eldest son to ensure that the "Special Yellow Retrievers" would continue to be looked after and improved. He knew how much his father loved these dogs and had already spent many days with them on the hills in the company of the Stalkers and Gamekeepers. Their reliability and enjoyment in the work that they had been trained to do would have been noted by him and he continued with the development of the breed for much of his life, ably assisted by those in charge of the welfare of the dogs on the estates at Guisachan and Edington.

Edward Marjoribanks was born on the 8th July 1849 at 4 Upper Grosvenor Street, London. He was the first child of Dudley Coutts Marjoribanks and his wife Isabella.

He followed in his father's footsteps in many ways but he was to achieve considerably more in his chosen career. From an early age there were plenty of household staff to look after his needs and it was not long before he had brothers and sisters to share his childhood. For his early education, private tutors came to the house. In September 1862 he went to Harrow School and like his father, had the headmaster at the time, Dr. Henry Montague Butler, as his teacher and housemaster. He left Harrow in 1865 and went to Christ Church College, Oxford. From the outset he was a popular student and a renowned sportsman and always ready to play a leading role in events at the school. His high spirits were to lead to a rather sudden end to his days at Oxford after what has become known as the "great library row". This centred on the dismissal of one of the porters who was popular with all the students, as he often turned a blind eye to some of their pranks. To have their revenge on several members of the staff, Edward and some other students, removed a number of statues from the library. They arranged them on the college lawns and lit bonfires between them causing some considerable damage - to the lawns and the statues. At first those responsible failed to own up but when the governing body of the university threatened to call in the police with a view to starting legal proceedings they decided it was time to confess. Edward, no doubt with firm pressure from his father was the first to apologise to the Dean. Despite this he was sent down, thus preventing him taking a degree. In private I have no doubt that his parents put it down as part of growing up and took some pleasure in their sons ill advised support for the dismissed porter.

In a perverse sort of way, Edward could have been handed out a mild punishment after being sent down, as in 1870 he was sent on a world tour, missing the shooting season at Guisachan and having to say goodbye for a time to Crocus, the yellow retriever that had been given to him the previous year by his father, who had bred him. I wonder what he missed most, the shooting or his dog? His tour started in America, from where he went on to Japan, China and

Photo 8: Edward Marjoribanks
(2nd Lord Tweedmouth)

India. He then went to Rome where it was planned that he would meet up with his parents. This arrangement had to be abandoned due to the outbreak of the Franco Prussian war. By the spring of 1871 Edward was home to his shooting and to Crocus. His parents were glad to see him back safely and the estate workers at Guisachan must have felt the same as by this time they had a great affection for this fine young man, who relished the days spent on the high grounds of the estate. The Head Gamekeeper at this time, Duncan MacLennan, was most pleased to see him return. Years later, Duncan related how they formed an excellent working relationship built on respect for each other. Duncan admired Edward's great accuracy with a rifle and his ability to learn quickly from all the experience that he himself had gained over many years. In return Edward showed kindness and respect to all those that he mixed with on the estate. He was also well liked by those who came to Guisachan as guests for the shooting season and there was one of these that he liked more than any of them. The guest list for the 1872 shooting season has an entry, written side-by-side, Edward and Fanny. The latter was Lady Fanny Octavia Louisa Spencer-Churchill. She was born on the 29th January 1853 and was the third daughter of John Winston Spencer-Churchill, the 7th Duke of Marlborough and his wife Lady Francis Anne Emily Vane. Her elder brother, Lord Randolph Henry Spencer-Churchill, born in 1849 was to become the father of Sir Winston Churchill.

It was in 1871 that Fanny had made her first visit to Guisachan. Ishbel, Dudley's daughter, said it was like having another sister, and within days they had a friendship that would continue throughout their life. Ishbel took great enjoyment in showing her the surrounding countryside and meeting the families of those who worked on the estate. Fanny had natural empathy with people and

Photo 9: Fanny Octavia Louisa Marjoribanks (nee Spencer-Churchill)
2nd Lady Tweedmouth, wife of Edward

was quickly accepted for her great charm and interest in everyone
and everything. It was not long before she met Edward. Not long
before he fell in love with her. Not long before they were engaged.
As Ishbel recorded - the perfect match. They had a love that was so
deep and admired that they went everywhere together, shared their

lives with everyone and when the time came, when death would part them, was to break the heart of the survivor.

Ishbel's "perfect match" was made even stronger by Fanny's love of the outdoors. By the time she met Edward she was an accomplished horse rider and had developed great skill with a rifle. These were qualities that were noted, by the Stalkers and keepers on the Guisachan estate, several of which had difficulty keeping up with her boundless energy and thorough zest for life. Added to this was her love of dogs. There is no doubt that the first time she visited Guisachan was also the first occasion that she saw a yellow retriever. Her future father-in-law would have delighted in showing her these favoured dogs and giving her the details of how well they worked on the hills. What she was told about them would have been proved when she went shooting with Edward accompanied by Crocus. Crocus was a firm favourite with Fanny and we are fortunate to have the portrait of her taken with the dog in 1876. Pupped in 1868, Crocus, is in a classic pose, sitting devotedly with Fanny, and showing the wonderful characteristics of the breed that have been retained to this day.

With the names of Edward and Fanny alongside one another in the Guisachan guest list for 1872 it is more than likely that by this time they were engaged. On the morning of 9th June 1873, a short carriage ride for Edward, from his father's home at Brook House, Park Lane, London and an equally short carriage ride for Fanny from her parents home at Lower Brook Street, Mayfair, London, brought them to St. James's Church, Piccadilly, where they were married. Ishbel was one of the bridesmaid's, her "perfect match" now complete. Unlike the rather low-key wedding of Edward's father's, this was a high society event with the guest list full of titled

Photo 10: Fanny Marjoribanks and Crocus, 1876
(by permission of the National Portrait Gallery)

Lords and Ladies. There was much comment from these and others as to how beautiful the bride looked in her white satin dress trimmed with lace and her bouquet of orange blossoms. She wore a necklace of pearls and a diamond pendant, which had been given to her by her future mother and father-in-law. Dudley had written to his son prior to the marriage in which on behalf of himself and his mother he congratulated him on choosing such a lovely wife.

After the wedding the bridal party went to the home of the bride's parents, where a large wedding breakfast had been arranged. The Duke of Abercorn proposed a toast for the newly married couple with best wishes for a healthy and happy marriage. Just before 2 o'clock they went by carriage to Waterloo Station and started on their honeymoon journey to Abbotsbury Castle, the home of the Earl of Ilchester. We will never know if Crocus went with them but if he did he may well have met up with his sister, Ada, who by now had been with the Earl since 1868. Crocus would have been more than happy but no doubt happier still would have been the bride and bridegroom but for different reasons! Their happiness was rewarded just nine months later, when on the 2nd March 1874; Fanny gave birth to a son, who was christened Dudley Churchill.

Edward and Fanny spent the first years of their married life at the London home, 134 Piccadilly, which Edward had acquired in 1874. He was called to the bar at the Inner Temple, London, in November of the same year. Although he was soon to be admired for the work that he did in the chambers of Sir John Duke Coleridge, a future Lord Chief justice, he did not get any satisfaction practising in law. His interests were turning more to politics, no doubt much to his father's delight. His first attempt to gain a seat at Westminster, standing for the constituency of Mid Kent, ended in defeat. He was to do better in 1881, when he was elected to succeed his father, who had been elevated to the House of Lords, as the Liberal MP for North Berwickshire. It was a seat that he was to hold until 1894, when on the death of his father he went to the House of Lords as the 2nd Lord Tweedmouth.

During the whole of this time Edward and Fanny were regulars at the shooting parties at Guisachan. On more than one occasion they stayed for over 6 weeks. Fanny was delighted to be back in the place were she had first met Edward. To her it was wonderful to be with the estate workers again, hearing all their news, visiting the school to see how the children were progressing and taking them gifts. The Stalkers and keepers were also pleased to see her, a Lady to them but equals to her. She truly loved the long days spent on the hills and in the glens with her husband and having the residents and the estate workers around her. She was often joined by her sister, Anne Emily, now the Duchess of Roxburghe after her marriage in 1874 to the 7th Duke, James Innis Kerr. They lived at Floors Castle, Kelso, along the River Tweed from Hutton Castle. They also had the dogs around them, the Yellow Retrievers including Crocus, and by now Edward's Red Setter, Sampson. This dog was used in a mating with Cowslip, sister of Crocus, in 1875, producing at least two yellow puppies, Jack and Gill. These were always listed in Dudley's studbooks as Edward's, and they went with him when Edward and Fanny took up residence at Duns Castle in 1877. Fanny welcomed going to Duns, situated eight miles north of the River Tweed and only six miles from her sister at Floors Castle.

With Edward having to spend quite a lot of time in London with his parliamentary work, it is interesting to see on the 1881 census that they kept memories of Guisachan with them. Among the servants was Louisa Mackenzie, who was born in Inverness and employed as Lady's maid to Fanny. The footman, Hugh Macdonald, was born in the parish of Kiltarlity, the same parish in which Guisachan is situated. At least they would have had regular news from north of the border. Although Edward had only been appointed as an MP in 1881, he was quickly picked out as being someone who would be of great benefit to the Liberal Party. Within a year he was appointed to the whips office. William Gladstone, the

Prime Minister at the time, had also noted how much Edward was respected by other members of the party, and the Prime Minister was among those invited to Guisachan in 1884 for the shooting season where he again saw how well Edward was regarded. No doubt, Fanny also charmed him and the guests!

Despite all the work that he was called upon to do in Parliament, his time spent in the constituency provided a regular and welcome break for both Edward and Fanny. From 1877 to 1883, when Parliament was not sitting, they stayed at Duns Castle. Edward's father did not forget them at this time and the stud book for 1883 lists 3 yellow puppies at the castle sent from Guisachan. Edward worked tirelessly in Berwickshire for the people, taking up their concerns for the area and travelling many miles to various meetings. He was always ably supported by Fanny, who took it upon herself to take charge of the needs of the womenfolk. With her natural kindness, she was admired for her genuine concern of others. As at Guisachan, she was treated as one equal to them.

During the 1880's Edward's workload increased markedly but with Fanny by his side they still managed to be at Guisachan for the shooting season. These gatherings were a time for them to meet up with friends, among them Ishbel, now Lady Aberdeen. Once again they were to spend days on the hills together enjoying the wild and open scenery. However, on one occasion, their happiness was marred when they were out riding with another guest, Miss Janie Ralli. While crossing a stream, which was partly flooded, her horse stumbled and Miss Ralli was thrown off, hitting her head on a boulder. By the time they managed to get her out of the water she was dead. Fanny, with her care and love for all those around her, was devastated and it took her a long time to get over this accident.

It was not however to stop her riding with gusto, and on more than one occasion, while riding with Edward, she came off her mount. One of these falls knocked her senseless. Edward must have feared the worst, when after ten minutes she was still unconscious. Urgent assistance was sent for but well before it arrived, she came round, and insisted on re-mounting her horse and returning to the house, passing those who had come to assist on the way. She wanted to get back, get changed and go with Edward to a constituency meeting that evening in Berwick on Tweed. From there they took the overnight train to London, for him to be in Parliament the next day, such was her great support for her husband.

In 1887, Edward and Fanny spent over two months at Guisachan for the shooting season and during this time close members of both families were again with them. Ishbel and her husband, John Sinclair Gordon, came for the same length of time. Her father, mother and sister, Sarah, were also there. At this time Edward had Jack and Gill, the yellow retrievers that were born in 1875 and had been trained at Duns Castle. The weather for this season was somewhat inclement and Fanny contracted a heavy cold, which she had difficulty in overcoming. Despite this she made sure that her guests were looked after and entertained during their stay. She was still unable to fully overcome her illness at the start of 1888, and on the advice of her physician, she went to America. She travelled with Edward and stayed for 4 months, during which time they visited Edward's brothers, Archie and Coutts. The brothers had been in America for nearly 10 years breeding cattle, being financed in this venture by their father, Dudley. Edward and Fanny returned to England in June, recommencing a busy schedule of political events in London and Berwickshire and by September they were back at Guisachan for the shooting season. The weather for this year was much better but Fanny, despite warnings from Edward to take more care while riding, suffered another heavy fall from her horse. It appears that she only rode a horse in one way - hard, fast and get there before anyone else! Recovery from this tumble took longer than she had hoped for and in early 1889 she went to Gastein, in Austria for specialist treatment.

On the 1891 census, Edward and Fanny were living at Ninewell House, Chirnside, Berwickshire with their son, Dudley Churchill, who had the somewhat unflattering occupation for someone of 17 years of age of "school boy". More appropriate would have been "Student at Harrow School." This sounds much better - and it is true! Also with them was Louisa Mackenzie, Lady's maid to Fanny. She must have looked after her Ladyship very well, as she was also with her in London in 1881. There is no doubt that yellow retrievers were with them also, as by this time the Edington Estate, which had been bought by Dudley in 1876 and extended to over 12,000 acres, had been developed into sizable shooting grounds. Much credit for this was given to the Gamekeeper, Thomas Weir Walker who had been appointed in 1881. He had reared the birds for the shooting season. He was provided with the dogs to retrieve the birds when they were shot.

Edward's days as an M.P. came to an end with the death of his father in 1894. Edward became the 2nd Lord Tweedmouth and within a short time, the Prime Minister, Lord Roseberry appointed him to the cabinet as Lord Privy Seal and Chancellor of the Duchy of Lancaster.

A year later an event took place that must have brought back memories to Edward of his days of high spirits while he was at

Harrow. His only son, Dudley Churchill, was named in a court case on a charge of breach of promise. This was in connection with an accusation that a proposal of marriage that he had made, had not been adhered to. The person who made the accusation was a chorus girl by the name of Birdie Sutherland. She was a comely, buxom girl but like others of her age who had appeared on stage was better seen only by gas light. The accusation alarmed both Edward and Fanny. They both agreed that she was not the type that they wanted their son to be involved with, despite the fact that she had an unblemished character. Ever the diplomat, Edward persuaded her to go abroad for a year at his expense, to study music with the very best tutors. If she felt the same about his son after a year he would agree to the marriage. Fanny was not taking any chances with this arrangement. As soon as Birdie had flown abroad she decided it was a good time to take her son to Canada to visit her great friend, Ishbel. Three months later Fanny returned, leaving Dudley Churchill in Canada. By this time the romantic passion of Dudley's first love had abated much to the relief of his parents.

After his father's death Edward and Fanny moved into Brook House. They also took over the running of Hutton Castle, on the Edington Estate and Guisachan where they continued to have visitors for the shooting season. The guest list was as varied as other years and in 1897 included the Duke and Duchess of York, the future King George V and Queen Mary. A Yellow Retriever, included in a photo taken of the guests for this year, shows what distinguished company these dogs liked to mix with!

Despite having no stud book at this time, there is plenty of evidence that Edward was using yellow retrievers on the estate at Guisachan and at Edington and photos of these still exist to support this. The shooting season was a time when Edward and Fanny could enjoy themselves, taking a more relaxed lifestyle, spending time on the hills and seeing old friends. Edward was welcomed back by the Stalkers and Gamekeepers. Fanny delighted in visiting the school again and being the perfect hostess to all around her. The time must have passed all too quickly for them and by the start of a new year they were back in London. On the 1901 census they are at Brook House and their son is with them, probably on leave, as by now he was a Lieutenant in the Royal Horse Guards. Of the fifteen house servants, three were from Scotland.

By the early 1900's Edward had reached high office in the government of the day. He was well liked by all around him, respected for his sound judgement, and always looking to improve the outlook and workings of the Liberal Party. However, he was soon to receive some devastating news. In May 1904, Fanny had to have an operation to remove a cancerous growth. She spent a week at Ascot to recuperate before returning to fulfil her busy schedule of social engagements. She accomplished these knowing, but only telling Edward, that the cancer had spread. In late July she left London for the last time and went to Guisachan. She wanted to say goodbye to the people on the estate that she loved so much. A place that was so special to her, the place, where she had first met Edward. With her husband by her side, she died on the 5th August 1904. Their 31 years of marriage, during which time they had shared so much, had supported each other and had been admired by so many, was at an end. Her death at the early age of 51 was a tragedy for Edward, a tragedy that he never recovered from.

The following day, her body was taken, by rail, from Beauly Station to Chirnside in Berwickshire. Large crowds turned out along the route to pay their respects. The funeral service took place two days later and was attended by relatives and friends and a large number of people who worked on the Edington Estate. Her death at such a young age, had come as a shock to all those who had known her.

Edward returned to London before the end of 1904. The gathering for the shooting season at Guisachan was cancelled. Edward attempted to immerse himself in his parliamentary work but financial problems, which had been mounting, were suddenly to get worse. For some time the business at Meux's brewery, of which he was a shareholder, had been steadily declining. He had to find money for his brothers, Archie and Coutts, whose cattle business in America was facing ruin. In order to raise money the shooting rights at Guisachan were sold to Lord Portsmouth. Very sadly for Edward this included some of the yellow retrievers. He also had to look at raising money on the Edington Estate, firstly by mortgaging part of it and then renting out the shooting. Despite their loyalty, which they still had for Edward, it was a worrying time for the workers on both estates. Duncan MacLennan, who had spent so many days with Edward on the hills since he was a young man, wrote later how sad it was to see him at Guisachan, on his own and visibly aged. The only thing that seemed to lift his spirits at this time was being back at the place were he had first met Fanny and having the yellow retrievers around him to provide some solace. The loving and sensitive nature of the breed must have noted the change as well.

In Parliament, although much changed, Edward was still seen as a skilful and respected politician but even these attributes were in decline. In 1905, the Prime Minister, Campbell Bannerman, appointed him 1st Lord of the Admiralty. He was seen to be someone whose persona and communication skills would be ideal to negotiate a resolution to the problem of an expansion of the German Navy while the British government was proposing cut backs. Edward was to come under severe criticism, for what was termed leaking information to the German emperor. Although later exonerated, Edward's judgement was called into question. He no longer had anyone to share the problems of state with. Fanny was no longer with him to give assistance.

In the summer of 1908 Edward suffered a heart attack. He was never to recover fully. His resignation from office followed in September 1908. Edward spent his last days being looked after by his sister Ishbel, now Lady Aberdeen at Phoenix Park, Dublin, the residence of her husband who was now Viceroy of Ireland. Edward died on the 15th September 1909.

Ishbel made all the arrangements for the funeral, which took place on the 20th September. She ensured that his final wishes were followed. His body was brought back to Chirnside, to be laid beside the person that he had loved so dearly. Since the time of her death he had paid for the restoration of the church. A full-length alabaster portrait of Fanny now adorns one of the inner walls. It is very beautiful, so much so that when seen it is not easy to take ones eyes from it. Outside, against the west wall, where his wife's body was interred, Edward had built a special memorial to her, an area where now he was laid to rest, now to be with her always. By arranging for this to be done, Edward had turned away from being interred in the family tomb at Kensal Green cemetery, London. He wanted to be forever in Scotland, the country he loved so much and to be with his beloved wife Fanny.

Dudley Churchill Marjoribanks, the only child of Edward and Fanny, became the 3rd Lord Tweedmouth. He had a distinguished career in the Royal Horse Guards. As a Lieutenant, he fought in the second Anglo-Boer war, after which he was awarded the Distinguished Service Medal and promoted to the rank of Lieutenant-Colonel. In 1901 he married Lady Muriel Brodrick and they had two daughters. When he died on 23 April 1935 the title became extinct.

In June 1905, Guisachan was sold to Lord Portsmouth. Hutton Castle and the Edington Estate were leased to Harold John Tennant MP in 1908. Dudley Churchill moved to Hutton Castle in 1911 and sold it to William Burrell, the ship builder and art collector in 1915.

Dudley Churchill did not carry on with breeding the Yellow Retriever. However by this time there were many others who had become enchanted by the breed and were to continue with its progress in the canine world.

Duncan MacLennan

Key
B - *Born*
M - *Married*
D - *Died*

John
B. 1806
D. 1883

— M. —

Margaret Sinclair
B. 1809
D. 1861

6 Sons

2 Daughters

Duncan
B. 1/8/1843 (Lochalsh)
D. 15/9/1927 (Guisachan)

M.
(Beauly)
28/11/1872

Jessie Kennedy
B. 1852 (Stratherick)
D. 7/5/1937 (Guisachan)

John
B. 1875

Maggie
B. 1878

Duncan
B. 1880

Annie
B. 1884

Malcolm
B. 1891

❦ 3 ❦

Duncan MacLennan

(1st August 1843 - 15th September 1927)

The Faithful Servant

DURING THE MIDDLE of the 19th century there was a considerable increase in the number of wealthy landowners who had made their fortune from the rapid expansion in commercial activity of the Victorian age. They set about purchasing and building large houses, often set in extensive grounds for their leisure time and to entertain and impress families and friends. This in turn provided employment for the local people, so that the estates functioned in an organised way. The popular pastimes of the gentry were hunting, fishing and shooting. It was in the autumn that the shooting season commenced and for the staff working on the forest hills and moors of the estates, it was the culmination of a year's work. They had to ensure that the grounds were well stocked for the shooting season. The landowners wanted the best sport for the guests who visited at this time of year. If this was not successful for those invited, it often meant that those responsible would be to blame and possibly replaced before the next year's shooting.

It was the Gamekeepers on the estates that were in charge of the rearing of the game birds. Where an estate covered high hills,

Deerstalkers were employed to ensure that the deer were always safe and well fed and also that the mating season had carried on without being hindered by any intruders onto the estate. Both the Gamekeepers and Stalkers relied on dogs and for these to be looked after properly kennel men and boys were employed. The dogs were looked upon as a very valuable asset to those out on the hills, working with them everyday and in all weather.

When Dudley Coutts Marjoribanks bought the estate at Guisachan in 1854, it was the responsibility of his Gamekeepers and Stalkers that he looked to, to provide the very best for the shooting season. A year after he acquired the grounds he appointed Simon Munro as the Head Keeper. In 1861, Simon took on a kennel boy by the name of Duncan MacLennan. He was to work on the estate until 1914, serving Dudley Coutts Marjoribanks, his son Edward and then Lord Portsmouth. All those who were employed were quickly immersed in the life at Guisachan and Duncan found that despite the short time that he had been there, he was treated as an equal. On Christmas Eve he was included in the annual shinty match, which took place on one of the fields near the main house. At the age of 17 he was well accomplished on the bagpipes. This was put to great use as he piped the teams on to the pitch before the competition. After the contest, as was the custom at this time, the servants and estate workers assembled in the kitchens below stairs, where a huge supper was laid on and once again Duncan provided some of the music for the dancing that followed. Within a few weeks he had been made to feel at home, which at this time, he was most in need of. A few months before he was employed at Guisachan, his mother had died. His father, John, who was a Shepherd, decided to take his 5 other sons and 2 daughters to New Zealand to start a new life. However, three of his sons were to

Photo 11: Duncan MacLennan and Jessie on their
Golden Wedding day 1922, with Lord Aberdeen (in kilt)

return to Scotland where they found work, either on or near the estate. For Duncan, Guisachan and the people on the estate were to be his home. At this early age he probably never thought he would spend the rest of his working life there, 48 years of which, he was to serve the Marjoribanks family.

On his first day as kennel boy - it must have been the first day! - Duncan would have met the dogs that he was to be in charge of. Dudley's stud list for 1861 lists 14 Pointers and 3 Deerhounds, so he was well occupied. Duncan, under the observant eye of Simon Munro, was quick to learn the skills required of a dog handler. He was also taught how to set the game in the early part of a year and was instructed in the correct way to stalk deer. Within a short time he had been appointed Under Gamekeeper and as a reward for his new position, was provided with a suit, made of Guisachan tweed. The pattern for this had been commissioned by Dudley Coutts in 1861 and still survives to this day, although the supply is now limited. As part of their conditions of employment, all Gamekeepers and Deerstalkers were provided with one suit a year. Duncan was also fortunate at this time to see the first Yellow Retriever at the kennels, with the arrival of Nous in 1865 and to have the Tweed Water Spaniels, Belle and Tweed. He also witnessed the first litter using these dogs with Crocus, Cowslip and Primrose born in 1868. Throughout this time there was plenty for Duncan to learn and plenty to keep him occupied.

On the 1871 census, he was living in the village at Tomich with his sister, Ann, who was 11 years younger. His occupation was given as Gamekeeper. Great sadness was to come to him and others on the estate in the midst of the 1873 shooting season, when the Head Gamekeeper, Simon Munro, died suddenly at the early age of 44. It

Photo 12: The Guisachan Gamekeepers
wearing Guisachan tweed (insert)
including Duncan MacLennan (pictured with telescope)

was a shock to all those who had worked with him on the hills and moors and to the visitors, many of whom had met him more than once. It was also a great loss to Dudley. Simon had been a loyal servant to him since the days when he had purchased Guisachan. Duncan knew that the person who had looked after him so well since he came to the estate was no longer there to turn to, for his valued words of advice. As a remark of respect to Simon, Dudley did not select a new Head Keeper for over two years. When he did, he appointed Alex McGillivray who was a year younger than Duncan. At the same time Duncan was made up to Gamekeeper.

When the news of Duncan's new position reached Edward he was more than pleased. Duncan had a natural affiliation with Edward, had instructed him about shooting and stalking and was respected by Edward and his new bride, Fanny. When time allowed they would all set off for long days on the hills, some of which rose to nearly 3,000 feet. What amazed Duncan on these excursions was that Fanny never tired. She could outpace him and other Stalkers, on the hills. When walking on the estate roads, Duncan chose to be on the grass verge so that she did not hear him running behind her. Another person who joined them frequently was Henry Hope Crealock. He was classed as a Journeyman Stalker, who travelled many miles in the highlands and stalked on all the largest estates. He was also a renowned artist and he drew some wonderful sketches, not only of other Stalkers but also the dogs which were with them. Among these are drawings of Crocus and one Crocus's sisters.

There is also a sketch of a rough terrier named Gruaga. This dog, which he kept in his pocket, belonged to Duncan Kennedy, another Stalker at Guisachan. The dog was used as a tracker, to assist in following the deer. This form of tracking had been passed down from Dudley, who had found it to be extremely effective. Keeping the dog in a pocket? Stalkers and Gamekeepers clothing had pockets in abundance and carrying a small terrier in a pocket, at waist height made it easier for the dog to pick up the scent and to survey the landscape. There was also another advantage. With a dog of this size in a pocket there was less chance of the handler falling over it!

On the 28th November 1872, Duncan got married at the Free Church at Kilmarock. His bride was Jessie Kennedy and they began their married life at Kirkfield Cottage in Tomich. In 1875 their first

Upper left: 'Crocus'
Lower left: Sister of Crocus
Lower right: 'Gruaga'
Kennedy's Little Tracker

Photo 13: The sketches by Lieutenant General Henry Hope
Crealock C.B. C.M.G. who visited Guisachan in 1875

son was born and christened John, after Duncan's father. In 1878 they had a daughter, christened Maggie and then on the 23rd September 1880 they had a second son, who was christened Duncan. In time this son also worked on the estate and benefited greatly from his father's experience and knowledge of the terrain.

In the stud book for 1880 Dudley lists a retriever by the name of Minos, with the added remark "with Duncan". The dam for this dog was Topsy, with the sire being Henry Meux's, Sambo. He may well have been entrusted with this dog, as by this time Crocus would have been past his working life. In 1882 Duncan has another retriever with him by the name of Saffron. In years to come, he was to have other retrievers listed in his care, one of which was Gill. This dog was from a litter by Edward's dog Jack, mated to a bitch, Zoe.

Duncan's loyalty and diligence in his work was rewarded in 1884, when he was appointed to the position of Under Stalker and four years later Head Stalker. With this appointment the family moved to Hilton House, a very elegant property to the south west of Guisachan. Although he would now be more in contact with the deer rather than the game on the estate, Duncan was to keep the retrievers that he already had, which was the acceptable thing on estates with different types of game. By this time there is evidence that he was also in charge of more dogs than the stud list kept by Dudley indicate. He could have been involved in breeding or at least rearing some of the litters. Having studied the lists kept by Dudley, I believe that he kept what he thought was the best of them, the others either going to keepers on the estate or estates very close to Guisachan. In 1889 Duncan had five puppies from a litter in the kennels adjoining Hilton House. Sadly a somewhat freak accident was to claim their lives. One Sunday Duncan and his family had gone to church leaving the puppies to be looked after by their daughter, Annie, who was born in 1884. While she was playing with them they all escaped outdoors. Being winter, the lake next to the property was frozen but not enough for the weight of five puppies and they all tragically fell through the ice and drowned. The young girl must have been utterly bereft and no amount of consoling from her parents would have helped her utter sadness as to what had happened.

Perhaps the birth of their next child did help Annie. In 1891, Duncan and his wife had another son who was christened Malcolm.

Photo 14: Painting of Duncan MacLennan
(by permission of Jessie Harrow)

A very good choice of name Duncan! And for myself I very much like the name of Annie!

When Duncan started work at Guisachan he never thought he would meet so many distinguished people, who were invited to the estate for the shooting season. There were plenty of Lords and Ladies, Dukes and Duchess's and Members of Parliament, even an American Senator, a Mr Philps. The Prime Minister of the day, Lord Balfour, was on the visitors list and future Prime Ministers, William Gladstone and Winston Churchill visited more than once. There were also people from the art world. Gourlay Steell, Sir Edwin Landseer and Henry Hope Crealock were regular guests. One would hope that the untitled and not so famous did not feel left out.

This includes plain Mr Cooper, Mr Compton and Mr Hughes. Despite their lack of title everyone was made welcome. On these visits it was Duncan's task to arrange for the various parties who wanted to join the shooting, into nimble and not so nimble groups! It would have been a cause of some embarrassment if someone put into the "not so nimble group" was taken onto the high grounds only to be carried back. At the end of successful day's shooting, the horses were used to bring back the deer and game that had been shot, these being strapped across the horse's back. It would have been rather unseemly if a titled or untitled visitor had to be included on the back of one of the horses as well!

Those who were invited for the shooting season often rewarded Duncan for all the care that he had taken during the time that they spent on the hills. A bottle of the finest malt whisky was presented to him by a grateful guest on more than one occasion. One of the visitors he remembered with great respect. His Grace, The Duke of Marlborough, accompanied by his three daughters, came for part of the shooting season in 1871. Duncan accompanied His Grace on the days shooting and he found him to be not only the perfect gentleman but very good with a rifle. The days on the hills with him were very successful with a number of stags shot cleanly. On his departure His Grace gave Duncan a purse of gold sovereigns with his sincere thanks for the time they had spent together in the deer forest.

The 1890's brought many changes to those who worked at Guisachan. Dudley, now Lord Tweedmouth, and his wife continued to visit, but like anyone that you do not see regularly, you notice when you see them again how they have aged. This was the case with his Lordship; and the sale of the prize cattle also was another indication that change was coming. Despite seeing a change in others, when the final day comes it is still a shock. So it was, when the news of the death of his Lordship reached Guisachan on the evening of the 4th of March 1894. Duncan was among many others who had worked on the estate throughout their working life. Within a short time after the sad news, thoughts turned as to what the future would bring and then the rumours started, with unfounded news circulating. Even Duncan was told he was to lose his job! I do not believe Duncan would have taken much notice of this and his faith in the Marjoribanks family was to be fulfilled. Within days of Dudley being laid to rest, Edward, now the 2nd Lord Tweedmouth and his much-respected wife, Fanny, went to Guisachan. The first visit they made was to Hilton House and they assured Duncan that his position as Head Deerstalker would continue, as would be the case with all the others employed on the estate. To confirm this further, within weeks plans were underway for the shooting season.

Photo 15: Hilton Lodge

In one other important aspect, there was to be no change - the "Special Yellow Retrievers" would still be at Guisachan - they also kept their job!

With the news that those employed at Guisachan would be kept on, their lives returned to some normality. The shooting season was again a time for guests to visit and the Christmas celebrations continued as normal. In 1897, Edward invited Duncan and Alick Fraser, who was now the Head Gamekeeper, to London, to see the celebrations to mark Queen Victoria's Diamond Jubilee. Edward paid all their expenses for the week. It was quite likely that this was the first time that either of them had visited London. They must have caught people's eyes, as they wore the suit of Guisachan tweed on their visit. Edward and his wife took them to the Houses of Parliament where they were warmly welcomed by several of the Lords who had visited Guisachan for the shooting season. It was Lord Radnor who gave them a guided tour of the chambers and in the dining room they dined with Lord Howe. The food must have been very good. When they went into the Commons to hear a speech, Duncan fell asleep, a trend that some MP's continue to this day! After their visit they were delighted to go and see the sights of London and to find their own way back to Brook House. That was the plan. They were never lost out on the hills at Guisachan, but they became lost in London! In those days if you got lost, you asked a Policeman for directions. The Policeman must have been somewhat taken aback to see these two weather beaten men in their tweed suits. He gave them directions but Alick Fraser was not so sure that he had been given the correct information and told Duncan of this, speaking in his native Gaelic. The Policeman laughed heartily. He had disguised his own native ancestry and then in the broadest Scots accent he gave them the right directions.

Duncan and Alick were much taken by the splendour of Brook House. They were generously entertained by Edward and Fanny and were made to feel very welcome. Years later, Duncan related how wonderful it was to be with them as guests, in the luxury of their own home, the same couple who enjoyed the long days on the hills. During the week they also went to Bath for the day, to visit the Dowager Lady Marjoribanks at her home in Prior Park. It was there that she showed them the room where Dudley had died. When the time came for them to return to Guisachan, Edward and Fanny provided them with a huge hamper of food and drink as provisions for the long journey north. I can imagine Fanny saying they'd have the basket back when they saw them later in the year at Guisachan.

The guests for the shooting season towards the end of the 19th century continued to comprise of Lords and Ladies from the highest level of society. The list for 1897 included royalty, with the Duke and Duchess of York, the future King George V and Queen Mary. On the first day that the Duke went shooting, Edward introduced Duncan to the future King. During the following two days Duncan was with him, and together with Edward, they shot three stags each on the first day and then seven each on the second and last day. Duncan related that his Royal Highness was a good shot. In deference to the Duke he never related how many he missed! A photo taken during this time shows a Yellow Retriever in the foreground, quite possibly the first time that the Duke and Duchess had seen this breed. On the final evening of his stay at Guisachan, Duncan was requested to go to the Duke's dressing room, where he presented him with an inscribed gold watch and chain, as a sincere thank you for organising such enjoyable days.

1901 marked the 40th year of Duncan's employment with the Marjoribanks family. During this time he had gained the highest admiration of those who worked with him. He was also respected by those who were invited to the estate during the shooting season. Throughout the whole of this time he had thoroughly enjoyed his work - and who would not - with the "Special Yellow Retrievers" around him. Nothing lasts forever and Duncan probably knew that changes would come but not all of them in the way that he expected or wanted. Financial problems were mounting for Edward which were not of his own making. The severest blow came to Edward, when Fanny died in 1904. Duncan had so many happy memories of her. The estate workers and the children were the same. She was admired and loved by everyone in a very special way. Within a year of her death, Edward decided to sell Guisachan. Duncan knew that this would mean a great change for him and others on the estate. They were once again wondering if they would have a job. Duncan was now 60 and despite all the experience that he had, there was no guarantee that he would find another position.

A potential buyer was Lord Portsmouth. He had known Edward's father for many years and had been a regular visitor to Guisachan during the shooting season. The sale took several months to be completed and during this time letters were sent between the Solicitors of both parties. Many of these disputed the value that had been made concerning the items of machinery that were used on the estate. Several of the dogs, at this time, are also mentioned in the letters including 2 Yellow Retrievers, Trixie and Brass, being within a total of 7 dogs. These were valued at £100. The valuation was accepted. Another letter lists Yellow Retrievers who were with the Keepers at this time, including Duncan and it was agreed that all were to remain with them. Lord Portsmouth also requested that his

Solicitors provided him with a list of all the employees on the estate and to their working value. The entry for Duncan tells us that he earned £50.00 a year, was provided with 1 suit of clothes, had a house rent free, was allowed 3 tons of coal and the "keep" of 2 cows. Although he was credited with being the Head Stalker, there is no mention of his value to the running of the estate. His son, who earned £45.00 a year, was provided with 1 tweed suit of clothes, was single and aged "about 24". He was credited as being a first class shot and an excellent trapper. Most of the other workers listed were given good reports, the words reliable and helpful being quoted more than once but spare a thought for Mary MacDonald, age "about 49" paid, when she was needed, 8 shilling a week. She "brushes leaves off the roads", seasonal work no doubt but there were quite a lot of roads on the estate! For all this, she was described as "not of much use". I have no doubt they would have missed someone who swept the leaves off the roads - particularly with all those trees! In June 1905 all those listed had a new employer, with Lord Portsmouth completing the sale for £60,000.

Guisachan was not the only shooting estate that Lord Portsmouth now owned. He also had Eggesford House at Wembworthy, North Devon and Hurstbourne Park at Whitchurch, Hampshire. At the latter property, the Yellow Retriever had been introduced as early as 1888. This was the year that Lord Portsmouth started to keep a list of his dogs and for that year he put down, "Flax, a present from Lord Tweedmouth." Flax never appeared on the stud lists that Dudley kept, which confirms that Dudley's lists only included what was at Guisachan at the end of each shooting season. Flax was a bitch, as the list for 1892 states "2 puppies bred, out of Flax by his Lordships dog, Tiger, and named Smut and Jet". With these names it is hard to imagine that these dogs were not black flatcoats. His

Lordship may not have liked what Flax had produced, as he sold Smut and killed Jet the same year. Flax could not have been that bad, as in 1894 she had another litter of 5 puppies by Captain Best's dog, although he did not name the Captains dog or his type. He gave one of these to Captain Best, one to "Edny Hayter" and he kept the other three and named them Fop, Floss and Fan. Lord Portsmouth kept his lists of dogs until 1925. For some of those years he lists 12 dogs and it is likely that some were bred and worked at Hurstbourne Park, while others were sent to Guisachan. With details also given as to where and to whom he gave them, the retrievers from the original Tweedmouth line were at this time leaving their Scottish roots. However, the pure bred lines were to remain north of the border for some time as there were also matings taking place at Edward's estate at Edington which was to belong to the family for some time to come.

Duncan remained in the service of Lord Portsmouth until 1914, when at the age of 70 he retired. He and his wife left Hilton House and went to live in the village at Tomich.

In 1922 they celebrated their Golden Wedding anniversary. There was a large gathering of family and friends, three of whom had attended their marriage in 1872. It was their eldest son, John, who on behalf of the family presented them with a special sovereign case, filled with money.

Duncan died on the 15th September 1927 at the age of 84. He was buried in the village churchyard at Struy, 6 miles north of Tomich. Among the pallbearers were his three sons, John, now factor of the Strathconon estate, Duncan junior who had taken over as Head Keeper at Guisachan after his father had retired, and Malcolm, the

Head Keeper at Kinloch Forest, Sutherland. The experience that he had gained as a Gamekeeper and Stalker over many years had been passed on to his sons and many others. He had been faithful to those who had employed him, no more so than the Marjoribanks family, whom on his own admission he would have given "his last breath for". He had had the wonderful experience of working and being with the "Special Yellow Retrievers" well before his death, had found new owners and new people who were to be captivated by these dogs. Their work was to carry on.

Thomas Weir Walker

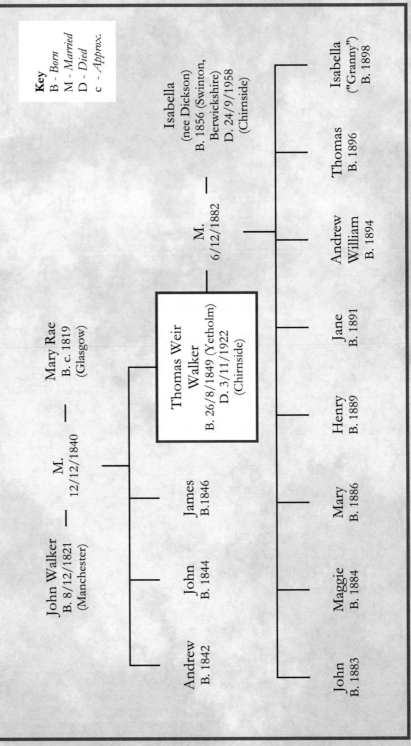

Key
B - *Born*
M - *Married*
D - *Died*
c - *Approx.*

Isabella
(nee Dickson)
B. 1856 (Swinton,
Berwickshire)
D. 24/9/1958
(Chirnside)

M.
6/12/1882

John Walker
B. 8/12/1821
(Manchester)

Mary Rae
B. c. 1819
(Glasgow)

M.
12/12/1840

Andrew
B. 1842

John
B. 1844

James
B.1846

Thomas Weir
Walker
B. 26/8/1849 (Yetholm)
D. 3/11/1922
(Chirnside)

John
B. 1883

Maggie
B. 1884

Mary
B. 1886

Henry
B. 1889

Jane
B. 1891

Andrew
William
B. 1894

Thomas
B. 1896

Isabella
("Granny")
B. 1898

❧ 4 ❧

Thomas Weir Walker

(26th August 1849 - 3rd November 1922)

A Well Known Character

T HE GUISACHAN ESTATE was not the only property that the
Marjoribanks family owned in Scotland. In 1876 Dudley
purchased the Edington Estate, seven miles west of Berwick on
Tweed. The terrain there was very different from that which the
family owned in Invernesshire. Covering 12,000 acres it was an area
of mixed agricultural land and there were grazing rights for a
number of tenant farmers. The appeal for Dudley, when he bought
it, was that he had ample shooting both on the uplands, which
climbed to almost 1,000 feet in places and on the lower ground,
where the game could be raised for the season. This area also
benefited Dudley, as it was in his parliamentary constituency of
Berwickshire. The purchase of the estate also included Hutton
Castle, dating from the early 13th century. He re-built the property,
adding an additional floor and erecting four castellated towers.

In the history of the development of Dudley's "Special Yellow
Retrievers", this is the estate, which has largely been forgotten but
from 1881 there were dogs from the kennels at Guisachan working
there. These in turn, needed someone to look after them and train

them. The person who was taken on for this work would, in time, show the same loyalty and trust to the Marjoribanks family that others had given. That person was Thomas Weir Walker.

Tom was born on the 26th August 1849, in Yetholm, Roxburghshire. His parents were married in Manchester in 1840, Tom's father, John, was born here and worked as a Joiner. Tom's mother, Mary nee Rae, was from Glasgow. Tom was their fourth son. His brothers, Andrew and James were born in Manchester and John in Liverpool. By 1851 their father had died and their mother was living in Yetholm with the children and she was listed on the census as a pauper. She may have gone to Yetholm to be close to other family members but no connection has been made so far. In 1861 Andrew is the only son still found in Yetholm, listed as an apprentice Shoemaker. James is in Rochester, Northumberland, also listed as an apprentice but with no other information as to a future occupation. This was revealed 10 years later! Nothing has been found for John or Tom, or their mother. On the census for 1871, with the exception of John, they are all living in Yetholm, with a family by the name of Young, and listed as boarders. By this time Andrew and James were both Shoemakers, - there's the answer for James - and Tom is a Gardener. Mary is not listed on this census. She could have died or re-married.

Yetholm in the 1860's had a large contingent of itinerant gypsies. They lived in what would today be classed as a suburb of the main town, called Kirk Yetholm. It was an area where the number of people would fluctuate, as the gypsies travelled many miles in all directions to find work. They were skilled and able to turn their hand to all tasks. They knew what to do and when, and any job they did was to a very high standard. When they returned home it was

Photo 16: A rare picture of Thomas Weir Walker

always to a neat and tidy cottage, in the best of which lived the Gypsy Queen. She was chosen by other gypsies living in the village. Their way of life and their knowledge of the countryside fascinated Tom. He saw how they caught rabbits and snared birds, a skill he remembered and turned to his own advantage, years later. Tom liked this way of life so much that he decided to run away with them. His brothers did not approve of this and set about rescuing him. After a few failed attempts, they seized their chance while several of them were getting water from the local well. Once they had captured Tom they took him home and no doubt gave him a good talking to. Whatever was said must have worked. Tom never ran away again.

When Tom was 14 he had the opportunity to assist on shooting days on the nearby estate owned by Colonel Wauchope. The greatest appeal to him in helping was to be on the land. The Gamekeeper who lived on the estate and came from south of the Scottish border was James Chandler, and Tom soon noted how well he had trained and worked the dogs, which were mainly Pointers.

When his school days ended, Tom took a job as a Gardener. He enjoyed the work but his days assisting James Chandler must have stuck with him and in 1874 he secured the position as Under-Keeper on the Floors Castle estate near Kelso, Roxburghshire. The Head Keeper was a Mr Wood, who had been there for 42 years. Tom was here for 4 years and on an estate of over 20,000 acres and with the help of Mr Wood, gained experience in all aspects of looking after game. It was during this time that he learnt how to hand rear pheasants and to look after the partridge and grouse. Dogs were on the estate with Pointers and Setters being worked. In 1878 Tom moved to the Ferneyhirst estate, near Jedburgh, owned by the Marquess of Lothian. He was again Under-Keeper answering to Mr William McCall. We will never know if Tom had been too well trained while he was at Floors Castle or if Mr McCall was too set in his ways to accept new methods in rearing the game but, after 10 months, Tom got the sack! I suspect he showed that, even at this early age, he was well advanced in dealing with game, as within two weeks he had gained employment on the Duke of Hamilton's Estate at Kinneil, near Bo'ness, Linlithgowshire. Here he worked alongside George Turnbull, the Head Keeper at the time. This estate bordered the Firth of Forth and although not large it had a very good reputation in providing excellent shooting in the season. Tom was happy in his work here but after eighteen months he received a letter from a friend advising him of a position as Head Keeper on an estate in the Scottish Borders. He discussed this with George, who strongly advised him to apply. Perhaps his friend knew whose estate it was! His interview took place at Duns Castle and for the first time he met Edward Marjoribanks. Perhaps Edward introduced the Yellow Retrievers to Tom that were at the castle at this time. If so, both Edward and the dogs gave their approval. Tom was appointed Head Keeper at the Edington Estate and he started work on the 1st February 1881. He was to remain here for 36 years, for much of that time working for the Marjoribanks family. He was to give very loyal service to his employee and worked with skill and diligence, and when the shooting season came Tom would ensure that the guests had excellent sport.

Tom compared the area of the Edington Estate as a deerskin spread out like a mat, with four projecting corners. Tom always resided in the North East corner, which meant that he often had to travel many miles to look after the game. At first he lodged on the estate with one of the tenant farmers, Henry Dickson, at Whiterig Farm.

He liked being there. He liked Isabella, Henry's eldest daughter, so much so that he soon fell in love with her. They were married on the 6th December 1882, a marriage that was to last for 40 years. Their new home was at Edington Hill Farm, two miles from Isabella's family.

When Tom started work at Edington one of his immediate priorities was to increase the amount of game for the shooting season, which in 1881 amounted to under 100 brace of partridge. There were very few pheasants at this time and little effort had been made to hand rear them, a situation that Tom was to change within a few years. In doing so, he had to consider the tenant farmers as these birds can quickly damage any seeds sown in the spring. The farmers had enough problems with the large rabbit population, which although they were a family source of food they also attracted poachers. The latter were to be a problem for many years. Tom, thanks to the gypsies, was well aware of the art of the poacher and the way they snare game. On many nights, especially in the breeding season, he was occupied checking the woods for intruders. With the assistance of the farmers, with whom Tom always kept good relations, and the police, many of the poachers were apprehended. The work could be dangerous. On one occasion Tom was shot in the hand and he was taken to Edinburgh Royal Infirmary where he had to spend three weeks with his hand in a salt bath. For a long time after this Tom had to wear a special glove while the injury healed. The problems with poachers, although seasonal, often ended with Tom having to appear at the local assizes in Berwick on Tweed, to give evidence. He was always grateful for the assistance that he had from the farmers who in turn were grateful to him for his consideration in their work and for his arrangements when visitors came for the shooting. Tom's efforts at increasing the

Photo 17: Hutton Castle

number of game were well rewarded and within a few years the days shoots were to total over four hundred head of game, with the number of pheasants shot being more than partridge. Dudley, now Lord Tweedmouth, and his son Edward, both of whom entertained guests at Hutton Castle, appreciated his success.

In 1883 Tom became a father - his wife, Isabella, giving birth to a son, who was christened John. Other children followed, with Maggie born in 1884, Mary 1886, Henry 1889, Jane 1891, who sadly died before she was one year old, Andrew 1894, Thomas 1896 and Isabella in 1898.

In my research of the people and places for this book, I was fortunate to meet the great grand daughter of Tom's daughter, Isabella. She remembers her "Granny" with great affection and often spoke about her childhood days with the dogs around her. I learnt where the kennels had been built for the Yellow Retrievers. Some of these came from Guisachan and others were bred there. At the time when my wife and I visited, the kennels were due to be demolished but there was some writing on the walls regarding the number of rabbits that had been shot. The outhouse, where only "the best food" was prepared for the dogs, was intact with its boiler still in place. Next to it was the bothy, which on the 1901 census was occupied by Duncan McGillivray, who was born in the parish of Kiltarlity, the same parish as Guisachan, and Robert Denholm born at Grantshouse in Berwickshire. Duncan was the son of Alex McGillivray who had been a Gamekeeper at Guisachan for over 20 years. It is more than likely that he came to Edington to look after a litter and to learn from Tom the training methods that he used with the young dogs. "Granny" also remembered a litter of nine Retriever puppies from America coming to the kennels in the early 1900's. None of these puppies, or those from other litters, were allowed into the house, the only exception being, when Tom was socialising them. This pleased "Granny" as puppies had a habit of peeing on the floor! On another occasion she remembered her father getting an urgent message to go to Berwick railway station to collect a box. When he got there he found that the box contained a rather wet and bedraggled puppy Irish Water Spaniel. Tom gave it a home but he never found out who had sent it! Was the person trying to pass it off as a Tweed Water Spaniel?

By the early 1900's Tom was recognised as a first-rate trainer and handler of the dogs in his care. Confirmation of this followed in an article entitled "The Best Dog for a Gamekeeper", published in The Gamekeeper Journal in 1901. This article provoked some fairly fierce reaction from a number of Keepers, with letters being

Photo 18 (Upper): The Kennels at the time
of our visit were partly dismantled

Photo 19 (Lower): The Outhouse where
food for the dogs would have been prepared

forwarded to the journal for over 6 months. These were to dispute the good and bad points of the dogs that the Gamekeepers used and for obvious reasons not all the letters gave the true name of the correspondent. One of these letters was from "A Head Keeper" - a great help! - extolling the virtues of the retriever breed introduced by Lord Tweedmouth. He even claimed that he would be sending a specimen to the Gamekeepers Dog Show of that year. This was held at Crystal Palace but on the show schedule no such dog was listed. Two months later a James Miller - thank you James for giving your name! - replied, saying how he was in full agreement with regards to the Retrievers of Lord Tweedmouth. He was writing from Twynholm in Dumfriesshire where he was working these dogs, having bought some from Lord Portsmouth. Despite the efforts of the journal to halt the letters in reply, they still came, with a Mr R Patterson claiming that the Tweedmouth Retriever was nothing but a mongrel! Shame on you Mr Patterson - wherever you were from! In defence of this came "Curly" with a letter the following month that gave the highest praise to Tom Walker. He had watched them being worked and assured Mr Patterson that they were the best working retrievers he had seen. Well written Curly, - wherever you were from! More praise for Tom came the following month, with "Celtic" agreeing with Curly's view and adding that Mr Patterson should make a point of seeing the Tweedmouth Retrievers at Muckross House, Killarney in Ireland, worked by Mr Chisholm, once a Keeper at Guisachan. Praise indeed for Tom from many people. These letters showed that by this time the Yellow Retriever was being established in places far away from their origins. Well done Tom - and what did you think of these retrievers? When asked he replied that they were "fine-tempered and good workers. I never found one hard in the mouth". He also clarified this somewhat by saying that like all breeds there were "noodles"

Photo 20: Tom Walker with his dogs

amongst them. That is excellent Tom: "noodles" are still with us today - I know, I have one!

The 1901 census, lists Tom at the Gamekeeper's House, Edington Hill, with his wife and 5 of his children. Their eldest son, John, died in 1897 after being bitten on the hand by a stray dog, the poison from the bite causing his death. As he had grown up with dogs around him it made his death an even sadder occasion. Their eldest daughter, Maggie, was in service at Hutton Castle. Despite a busy working life, Tom still found time to tend to his sizable garden. He was as skilled with growing vegetables as he was in training dogs. On more than one occasion he won prizes at the annual Chirnside fete. This was always well attended and Edward and his wife, Fanny, were there to present the prizes. Tom was also a skilful draughts player and was frequently on the winners lists when tournaments were held at Chirnside and the local villages. He liked a drink - but only during two weeks of the year! This was after the pheasants and partridges had been reared for the shooting season. Then it was off to the Waterloo Arms in Chirnside every day, for two weeks. At all other times he never drank and remained sober.

Unlike the shooting at Guisachan, a visitors list has not been found for those who went to Hutton Castle, although one of those was certainly the Liberal M.P. Harold John Tennant, with whom Tom was to have a close working relationship in years to come. As at Guisachan, 1904 was to be the year that a gradual change would come to those working at Hutton Castle and the Edington Estate. The death of Lady Fanny Tweedmouth affected them all. They were no doubt humbled and, in a strange way, honoured that she chose to be laid to rest at Chirnside. Her husband built a fitting memorial to her in the churchyard and I have no doubt that Tom and his wife, who regularly attended church, would have paid their respects as they passed the memorial on their way to Sunday services. When Edward was interred beside her in 1909 it brought to an end twenty-eight years of loyal service that Tom had given to the Marjoribanks family.

Tom reached his 60th birthday the same year that Edward died. By this time he probably would have not wished to find another position and to move from an area where he was very well liked. The estate was left to Dudley Churchill, the only son of Edward and Fanny, who now assumed the title 3rd Lord Tweedmouth. He had chosen a military career and did not move into Hutton Castle. Within less than a year of his father's death he leased the property and the shooting rights to Harold John Tennant. By now he was well known to Tom Walker, and the workings of the estate did not change for some years to come. The breeding of the Retrievers carried on at Edington and also on the adjoining Manderston estate. The Gamekeeper here was John Simpson and in 1916 he advertised puppies for sale as "pure Tweedmouth strain" - so we know where they came from - "exceptional nice puppies" - what else! - "grand colour" - and so they should be - they were advertised as none other than Golden Retrievers. So time was moving on. The annual shoots also carried on and by now, when the shooting season came the number of game had increased significantly from the time when Tom went to work at Edington. By 1911, Tom was passing his wide knowledge of keeping game onto his sons, Henry and Thomas. Not to miss out, his youngest son, Andrew, was kennel boy. Isabella, now 12 years old, was still at school. I have no doubt that she assisted and loved having the dogs with her.

The outbreak of the First World War in 1914 was to add to changes that were to affect large parts of the country. Many Gamekeepers signed up to serve the country, many of who did not return. I have not been able to find out if any of Tom's sons enlisted but I do know that if his son, Tom, did serve, he returned safely, as in 1923 he was the Gamekeeper at the Ayton Castle Estate, 5 miles east of Edington. As the war continued and at times it seemed to be never ending, the sport on the estate diminished and the time spent on it by Tom's employer lessened due to his parliamentary work in London. Tom took this opportunity to keep Harold Tennant informed of what was happening on the estate throughout the war years. Harold valued these letters, so much so, that at the end of 1918, he published a book entitled "Letters from a Lowland Keeper". This book, now difficult to obtain, gives a wonderful insight of conditions on the estate at the time. Harold commented in the book about how considerate Tom was to provide him with news that was to act as an escape from his parliamentary work in London. Harold also related how much he appreciated Tom's very kind letter that he sent to him after hearing that his son, Henry, had been killed in France on the 27th May 1917, at the age of just 20. Tom had spent many days on the estate with Henry teaching him how to shoot and to bring down the game cleanly. The book also includes the wonderful photo of Tom with some of his Retrievers. I believe that the one in the left hand corner, as one looks at photo 20, is Brass, a favourite of Tom's. He was the only one allowed to sleep in the house. Second from the right, looks like a noodle! Well it does look like a dog that I know very well! In the centre is a Sealyham, - "Granny" confirmed this - possibly used in controlling the rabbits. Tom himself belies his 6-foot stature but look carefully and one can see his gloved left hand, which he always wore when out working following the shooting incident in the 1880's. The bowler hat - or billycock as some Gamekeepers called it - he is wearing is not for the sake of a good photo. Gamekeepers often wore these as a form of crash helmet, to protect them from attack by poachers.

In 1916 Tom retired and went to live at Hillside Cottage in Chirnside. The view from this cottage is spectacular. To the south on a fine day you can see the Tweed twisting and turning for miles along the valley below. Beyond this the Northumberland Hills stretch for miles in a wide arc from west to east and on the finest of days Holy Island can be seen, surrounded at times by the North Sea. On the not so fine days Tom could turn north and a short walk up the hill and he was at the Waterloo Arms! An occasional drink now, not his annual two weeks celebration of his younger days!

By this time Tom was deaf, a problem that appeared to be in the family line. His elder brother, Andrew, also known as Wally, had gone totally deaf at the age of 11 after contracting measles. Tom had plenty of time to reflect on the service that he had given so diligently to those who had employed him and he had had over 30 years working with the Retrievers, no doubt just as special to him as those who had gone before him. In his spare time he also composed this wonderful poem.

❦ Tae Keep a Clean Sheet ❦

As we travel through life wi' oor troubles and cares
We shouldna forget that others hae their's,
And tae gie a bit of help tae the needy we meet
Will help ane another tae keep a clean sheet.

Tho' the sun may be shining and a'thing look fair
We should ever be stapping wi' caution and care
It's sae easy tae stumal and slip off oor feet,
And add a wheen mair dirty spots tae oor sheet.

It's right tae hae pleasures, but let us think twice
Some pleasures and cantrips require a high price;
Yet tae look unco-guid and very discreet
Is often the time we get spots on oor sheet.

Let's look at things right and oor conscience will tell's
If we're faithful tae others we're true tae oor sell's
Let's aye keep in mind, tho' very discreet
It's a gey kittle job tae keep a clean sheet.

Tom died on the 3rd November 1922. He was buried in the graveyard at Chirnside. His headstone shows that with him is his daughter, Jane, who died before she was one year old. He had to wait over thirty years before his wife joined them, being laid to rest in 1958 at the age of one hundred and one. Their son Andrew was also buried here in 1964 at the age of seventy.

The contribution that Thomas Weir Walker made to the development of the Yellow Retriever should not be underestimated. He was undoubtedly an excellent handler and trainer and he was true to the breed throughout his time at Edington. He was well respected and trusted by the Marjoribanks family. His working relationship with Mr Harold Tennant was on the highest level. Other Gamekeepers held him in great esteem and on the estates that bordered the Tweed, the Yellow Retrievers were being used and their ability as a reliable working breed was increasingly recognised.

Photo 21: Tom Walker's headstone with
my dogs, Tessa (left), and my dear "noodle" Lucy (right)

Donald Macdonald

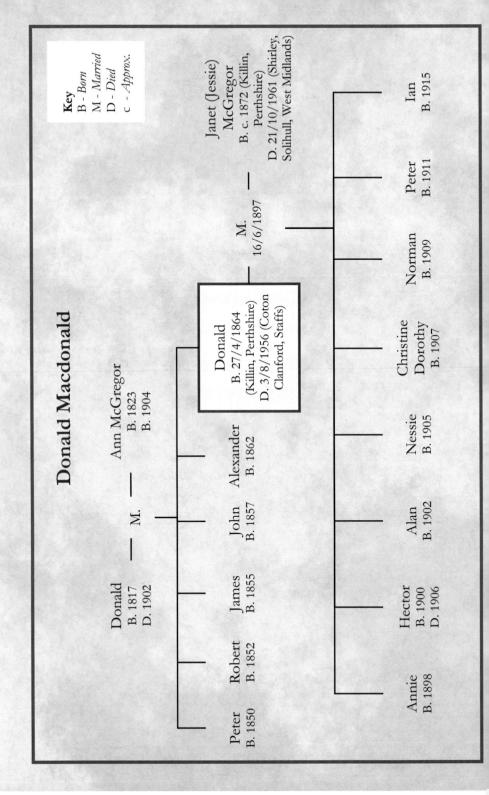

Key
B - *Born*
M - *Married*
D - *Died*
c - *Approx.*

Donald
B. 1817
D. 1902

— M. —

Ann McGregor
B. 1823
B. 1904

Peter
B. 1850

Robert
B. 1852

James
B. 1855

John
B. 1857

Alexander
B. 1862

Donald
B. 27/4/1864
(Killin, Perthshire)
D. 3/8/1956 (Coton
Clanford, Staffs)

M.
16/6/1897

Janet (Jessie)
McGregor
B. c. 1872 (Killin,
Perthshire)
D. 21/10/1961 (Shirley,
Solihull, West Midlands)

Annie
B. 1898

Hector
B. 1900
D. 1906

Alan
B. 1902

Nessie
B. 1905

Christine
Dorothy
B. 1907

Norman
B. 1909

Peter
B. 1911

Ian
B. 1915

❧ 5 ❧

Donald Macdonald

(27th April 1864 - 3rd August 1956)

Dedicated Keeper and Showman

B Y THE EARLY 19th century the Yellow Retriever was being recognised as a worthy addition to other breeds of gun dogs. Their popularity had increased to such an extent that initial prejudice towards them was a thing of the past. Gamekeepers who had trained them quickly recognised their merits, knew how willing they were to please their handler and showed a loyalty to them that was unsurpassed by other gun dog breeds. In was also the time when the Gamekeepers were looking to show their dogs. At Crufts and other organised events around the country the keepers found that there were far too many classes for what they politely termed as "dainty dogs". This was brought to the attention of the Gamekeepers Association and agreement was reached to hold a show specifically for gun dogs and keepers. The first of these was held at Crystal Palace, London in 1900. It took place at the start of August and two hundred and three dogs were entered. The largest entries were for Retrievers, with the Flat Coat the most popular. There were also classes for Curly Coated Retrievers, Spaniels, Clumber & Field Spaniels, Pointers, Setters and Labradors; although there was just one class for this breed. The show was also a time when the keepers were allowed to buy and sell dogs, with a small amount of the sale going to the organisers of the event. This was of use to Keepers, who either had too many dogs or not enough trained for the shooting season, which started within days after the show took place. The first show was a huge success. The entries far exceeded what the association expected and the number of dogs shown in all classes surprised everyone. There was general agreement that an event of this type should be held every year. A request was made to the Gamekeepers' Association committee that the show should be held in the month of March. This would coincide with the time when the workload on the various estates was not as great as other times in the year. For dogs, which changed owners at the show, there would be more time for them to spend with their new handlers prior to the start of the shooting season in August. There was also a request that the show should be held at different venues around the country. These requests were all approved and year on year the entries and numbers of dogs at the shows increased. The show for 1910 held at the Corn Market, Shrewsbury was the best. It was the first time that Yellow Retrievers, as they were classed at this annual event, were shown at the Gamekeepers show. The Keeper who showed them was Donald Macdonald. His surname is not mis-spelt. His Great Grandson has confirmed that this is the way that Donald spelt it, and as he was the person who did so much to increase the popularity of the breed, there is no way I am going to change it!

Donald Macdonald was born on 27th April 1864 at Killin, Perthshire. Both his father, also named Donald, and his mother, Ann, nee. McGregor, were born in this part of Perthshire. Donald, Senior, was a Gamekeeper, working for the Campbell family on the Breadalbane Estate, a position that he held for 37 years. Donald

Photo 22: Donald Macdonald

Junior was the youngest of six sons. Of the others, Peter born in 1850 died at the early age of seventeen, Robert, born in 1852 went to New Zealand, James, born in 1855 went to Western Australia, where he worked on the railways, being the first station master at Coolgardie. This was at the time when the line was opened to transport workers and equipment to the goldfields. Alexander was born in 1862 and worked as a gardener. The fourth son, John, born in 1857, followed his father's occupation and by 1880 he was living at Tressady, near Rogart, in the County of Sutherland, on a shooting estate owned by the Duke of Sutherland. The 1881 census lists Donald as unemployed, living with his parents at Lochlee, near Forfar, in the County of Angus, another part of the Breadalbane estate. With his father and elder brother both Gamekeepers it was not surprising that Donald chose to follow the same occupation and, for a while, to follow in his father's footsteps. On the 1891 census, Donald Senior was now retired, Donald Junior's occupation was recorded as Gamekeeper and he was living with his parents at Lochlee.

Both Donald and his father had Flat Coat Retrievers to assist them in their work. I have no doubt that John also had them. With John working on an estate 30 miles north of Guisachan, it is more than likely that he knew of the Yellow Retriever. By 1895, the Strathconon estate, which is between the estates of Guisachan and Easter Ross, where John worked, had a sizable number of Yellow Retrievers. The Strathconon estate belonged to Captain Coombe. The Coombe family were part owners of the London brewers, Watney Coombe Reid, very convenient for the Marjoribanks family, who were very much involved with the Meux's brewery. No doubt they met each other on more than one occasion for a beer tasting session!

In 1897, Donald met a young lady by the name of Janet McGregor. All her family were born in Killin and on the 16th June 1897 they were married. Despite both of them being born in Perthshire, it was not long before they moved from the area. In 1898 they were living in the parish of Ewes in Dumfriesshire, where Donald had taken a position as a game guard on an estate owned by the Duke of Buccleugh. It was here that their first child, a daughter named Annie was born, on the 20th of May 1898. Not long after this they moved to Keith Hall in Aberdeenshire, where on 7th February 1900 their first son, Hector was born. The family were on the move again a year later, and this time it was away from Scotland. Donald went to work as Head Keeper on the Ingestre Estate in Staffordshire owned by Charles Henry Chetwynd-Talbot, the 20th Earl of Shrewsbury. He was to work here until he retired, 32 years later.

The Ingestre Estate covered over 12,000 acres to the east of Stafford. Donald succeeded the previous Head Keeper, John

Photo 23: The Ingestre Keepers

White, who due to ill health had to retire. To obtain its full shooting potential, the estate needed a lot done to it, and with the full agreement of the Earl, Donald set about modernising the breeding of both the deer and game birds. To assist him, the number of keepers that were on the estate when he came there was doubled from 6 to 12. A programme of hand rearing birds was introduced. Any excess in the number of birds bred were sold to other estates. The money received from these sales was used to continually improve the breeding of the game and as a result, the quality of the shooting.

Donald was provided with a large house with 7 rooms, which was more than suitable to accommodate his growing family. Alan was born in 1902, Nessie in 1905, Christina Dorothy in 1907, Norman in 1909, Peter, in 1911 and Ian in 1915. Donald and Jessie experienced family sadness during this time. In 1906 their first children, Annie and Hector, contracted Diphtheria and both were admitted to hospital. The disease was widespread at this time and children of other families in the area were also in the hospital. Hector's condition improved after a few days and as an act of kindness, he assisted another boy in the hospital by fetching him a glass of water and extra pillows. Unexpectedly the following day, 1st February, Hector died. Annie recovered, but must have been very saddened at the loss of her brother but no doubt rightly proud of her brother, putting others first at such an early age.

From the early 1900's Donald was an active and keen supporter of the Gamekeepers' Association. In 1903 he was elected to the committee. The main objective of the association was to ensure that the working conditions for all keepers was respected and adhered to by the landowners who employed them. Although at this time there were no statutory wage rates for keepers, the association acted as an authority to ensure that they were given a fair wage and the correct living accommodation. As the dogs played a vital part in their work, they made sure that the keepers were paid for their upkeep, and that they were provided with the correct conditions for the dogs to live in, and the right food. In general, most landowners respected and provided this, but there was always a small minority that did not show consideration to their employees or the dogs. If this was the case the association was there to remedy the situation. They were also there to provide financial help to the widows of Gamekeepers who were killed while carrying out their work. Sadly this was not a rare event. Quite often it would happen while apprehending poachers, but there were others times when an accident happened with the keepers own rifle. At most times the landowners provided ample assistance when tragedy came to the families of keepers. When they did not have assistance, the association was there to help, and in some cases they started court proceedings against the landowners to ensure that proper financial support was given to the relatives.

Donald was mindful of the problems that keepers had to cope with, but apart from a few minor cases of poaching there were no real problems during his time at Ingestre. He had an excellent working relationship with The Earl and the Countess, both of whom enjoyed the shooting season and were excellent shots. They respected Donald for the work that he did especially the way he organised the other keepers to provide the best shooting, when guests of The Earl and his wife visited. Unfortunately, no visitor lists during the shooting season have been found, but in 1907 King Edward VII was amongst the guests and stayed for a few days. He was well pleased with the number of game that he bagged despite the foggy weather, which on some days was a hindrance. Perhaps some of the time was spent calling to the birds - where are you!

When Donald went to Ingestre he brought with him a number of Flat Coat Retrievers. This breed was already being worked on the estate, as early photographs show. He was also looking to breed his own dogs for the future. These were not to be confined to Flat Coats. Nothing wrong with the breed, but like others before and after him he was already smitten by another breed. You may have guessed - it was the Yellow Retriever! By the 1900's a registration system for identifying owners and breeders of pedigree dogs was being introduced by the Kennel Club. The benefit of this system was that owners were able to have a record of the sire and dam of the dog that they purchased, and that the breeder was able to track further mating from the dogs that they had sold on. The affix that a breeder chose was of their own choice but in the early 1900's they often selected the kennel that they came from or the area. A chosen affix could, at this time, be used for more than one breed. Once they had purchased a dog they were at liberty to register it under their own affix, or if it had already been registered, have it changed to their affix. Donald was among the first owners to apply for an affix, and no doubt after a lot of thought, he chose, Ingestre! His name first appeared as an owner on the registration list of 1904 with Ingestre Lucy, a Flat Coat, purchased from a Daniel Crewe. As a breeder, Donald's name was first recorded in 1906 when Ingestre Lucy had a litter of Flat Coats. He kept one bitch and registered it as Ingestre Nora. Three weeks later he brought his first Yellow Retriever to the kennels at Ingestre. This dog was bought from a Mr W Harrington and Donald registered it as Ingestre Scamp. He continued to add to the number of Yellow Retrievers at Ingestre and was soon breeding from them. The bitch that he used was

Photo 24: Donald's young dogs
(Shrewsbury Show 1912)

Ingestre Tyne, born in 1905, and bought from a Mr Hunter. From a litter out of Ingestre Scamp and Ingestre Tyne he kept one of the dogs and registered it as Ingestre Dred. Donald was well pleased with the first Yellow Retrievers that he now had at Ingestre, and he showed Scamp at Crufts in the class for Golden Retrievers in 1909 winning a 3rd place in the class for open dogs and bitches. Two months later he took Scamp and Dred to the Gamekeepers Dog Show at the Corn Market, Shrewsbury, where in the same class for Yellow Retrievers, Dred took first place and Scamp was second. These were the first Yellow Retrievers to be exhibited at an official Gamekeepers Dog Show.

By 1914 the number of Yellow Retrievers working at Ingestre had increased to 12. Donald had bred all of these. Puppies from the litters that he bred had been bought from him, and in time were worked on other estates. Donald's breeding continued to add to the popularity of the breed, not only as a working dog but also at shows. He continued to support the Gamekeepers Shows and Crufts, and his most successful dog during this time was Top Twig, which was placed on several occasions. He also entered some of the major shows around the country, becoming a true ambassador for the breed. He entered the major shows at Richmond, Birmingham, and Manchester, and he was often placed in one or more classes. On October 17th 1913 he was at a show in Edinburgh, where it was reported "there was a fine show of Goldens". This could possibly have been the first time he ventured north of the border since taking the head keepers appointment at Ingestre. Donald also won some sponsored prizes, with a Trophy being awarded to him at the Newcastle Dog Show in 1911, and at the Norfolk Game Show in 1916 where he won 1 cwt. of Meal Biscuit for the best golden. When news of this got back to the kennels at Ingestre there must have been huge celebrations among the dogs! I have no idea how Donald managed to get his prize back to Staffordshire.

In addition to prizes that Donald won at the dog shows, he also attended shooting competitions that were held locally. These were organised by the Clay Bird Shooting Association, which today is known as the Clay Pigeon Shooting Association. Donald was successful at these events on more than one occasion and in 1912 he was awarded with a very elegant engraved Trophy at the Championship show sponsored by the shooting journal, The Field. This Trophy has been passed down through the generations of Donald's family. It is a valued memory of what he achieved in his working life.

The shooting season was the time that The Earl and Countess would always be at Ingestre Hall with their invited guests. Donald had worked hard to improve the potential for shooting on the estate, and all those who were invited were well satisfied with the results. At other times in the year, the Earl and Countess were in London. Having succeeded to the title at the early age of 17, and being left a house in Portland Place, it is more than likely that the bright lights of London were of more appeal to them outside of the shooting season. With The Earl out of sight, Donald could, within reason, choose to show his dogs, much to the benefit of the breed. He was also able to make some money out of selling some of the puppies that he had bred and in addition to this he was paid for game that were shot out of season. Although a visitor's list has never been found for the Ingestre shooting season, what has survived, and is of interest, are the diaries of William Towers Mynors, the Private Secretary to The Earl for many years. Among the entries, covering over 15 years, are the amounts paid to Donald for game. It includes 1 shilling paid for "a couple of little rabbits" - it does not say if these were for pets or the pot! - 7 shillings and sixpence for 3 brace of headless pheasants, 13 shillings and 6 pence for 3 brace of pheasants - that seems a bit pricey, a difference of 6 shillings just to leave the head on! - 12 shillings for Rabbits - it does not say how many but it was in 1907, and I have not been able to find out what the going rate for a rabbit was at this time. Money was also paid to Donald for Wood Pigeons, Wild Ducks, a Hare and for some Venison.

Like other shooting estates in the British Isles, Ingestre was increasingly feeling the effects of the 1st World War, and by 1916 there was a problem in finding workers. Over half of all Gamekeepers in the country had enlisted. Although they were enthusiastic to serve, the Army welcomed them, as most of them were already trained to use a rifle. Without the labour force the breeding of game faltered and the number of people who were able to come to the estate for the shooting season fell. At the end of 1917, a large part of Ingestre Hall was given over as a hospital for wounded soldiers mainly from the Anzac regiments. Donald also withdrew from breeding dogs and attending shows. When the war finally ended there was only a slow recovery from the devastation that it had caused. It was estimated that nearly half of all the Gamekeepers who had enlisted had either failed to return or were so badly injured that they could not return to their previous occupation. With the country largely bankrupt, the shooting estates were not able to function in the way they had only 4 years before. The Gamekeepers' Association were foremost in providing support to grieving families of keepers, killed in action. To assist them with this, they turned to Donald who willingly took the position of Chairman in 1920.

A year later, the Earl of Shrewsbury died at the age of 61. As was often the tradition Donald and other Gamekeepers acted as pallbearers at the funeral. He was laid to rest in the church, just yards from the main house. It was a nephew, John Chetwynd-Talbot, who succeeded to the title of 21st Earl. He had little in the way of finance to assist in restoring the shooting on the estate. It is also questionable if he had the interest in the estate. Inevitably this led to parts of the grounds being sold off. Donald faced problems with lack of staff, especially with the rearing of game birds. His time was also limited in breeding dogs and it was not until 1922 that a bitch named Ingestre Rajah was born. It would be another 2 years before this dog was registered with the Kennel Club. Although

Photo 25: Donald and family 1902

Donald was the breeder, there is no indication as to how many dogs there were in the litter.

In 1928, Donald relinquished his chairmanship of the Gamekeepers' Association. They in turn were quick to congratulate him on all the work that he had done throughout some very difficult years. Donald retired to Walton-on-the-Hill, Staffordshire in the 1940s. He and his wife moved to Coton Clanford (2 miles north of Haughton) in the 1950s to be with, and to be cared for by, their eldest daughter Annie. It was here that Donald spent his last days, filled with memories of his work, and for a lover of the Yellow Retriever there were many memories. It was also time spent reading, including his favourite poem:

Listen Carefully to Me

Never, never let your gun
Pointed be at any one
That it may unloaded be
Matters not the least to me

When a hedge or fence you cross
Though of time it cause a loss
From your gun a cartridge take
For the greater safety sake

If, you and neighbouring gun
Bird may fly, or beast may run
Let this maxim e'er be thine
Follow not across the line

Stops and beaters oft unseen
Lurk behind some leafy screen
Calm and steady always be
Never shoot where you don't see

Keep your place and silent be
Game can hear and game can see
Don't be greedy, better spared
Is a pheasant, than one shared

You may kill, or you may miss
But at all times think of this
All the pheasants ever bred,
Won't repay for one man dead .

One day, while looking at the fire in his cottage he was asked what he was doing. His reply was, "waiting for death to come down the chimney". That day came on the 3rd August 1956. A few days later he was buried in the churchyard at Ingestre, a fitting resting place, on the estate, where he had worked for so many years. He was 92. On the 21st October 1961, his wife died and was laid to rest with him.

During his working life, Donald had mixed with people from all levels of society. They all spoke well of him, respected him for his outgoing personality and his skills as a Gamekeeper and dog handler. He had brought the Yellow Retriever to dog shows and shown how well they could be worked. He had brought recognition of the breed and had witnessed the breed's title change to Golden Retriever. For many people in the dog world, this would continue to add to their increasing popularity. His living relatives should be more than pleased with Donald's legacy.

Lewis Vernon Harcourt

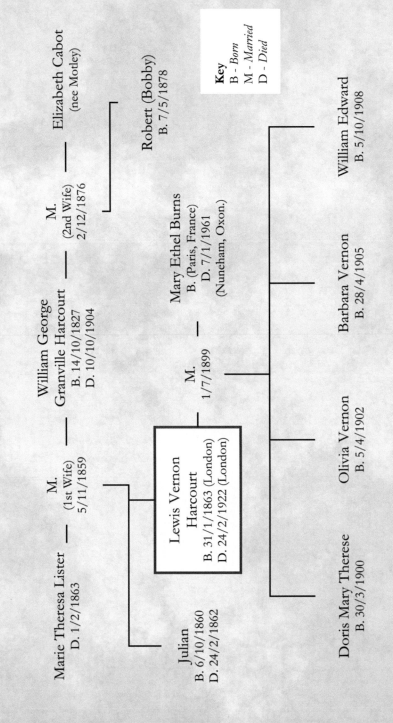

Key
B - *Born*
M - *Married*
D - *Died*

Marie Theresa Lister
D. 1/2/1863

M.
(1st Wife)
5/11/1859

William George
Granville Harcourt
B. 14/10/1827
D. 10/10/1904

M.
(2nd Wife)
2/12/1876

Elizabeth Cabot
(nee Motley)

Robert (Bobby)
B. 7/5/1878

Julian
B. 6/10/1860
D. 24/2/1862

Lewis Vernon
Harcourt
B. 31/1/1863 (London)
D. 24/2/1922 (London)

M.
1/7/1899

Mary Ethel Burns
B. (Paris, France)
D. 7/1/1961
(Nuneham, Oxon.)

Doris Mary Therese
B. 30/3/1900

Olivia Vernon
B. 5/4/1902

Barbara Vernon
B. 28/4/1905

William Edward
B. 5/10/1908

❦ 6 ❧

Lewis Vernon Harcourt
(31st January 1863 - 24th February 1922)

Winning Gold

T HE GUISACHAN VISITORS list for the shooting season
contains fascinating details of people, from various walks of
life, who accepted their invitation from the Marjoribanks family.
Some stayed for a week and others for up to three weeks and some
made more than one visit in the season. Their hosts would be there
for most of the time, only a family wedding would get in the way!
At this time of year the estate was very busy. There were daily
arrivals and departures, and added to this were the many suppliers
who brought provisions to keep the visitors well fed. With both
Dudley and his son being members of Parliament for many years it
is not surprising that a number of MPs were invited. In 1869 one of
these was William Vernon Harcourt. He came on the 6th of
September and stayed for a week. At this time William was the
Liberal Member of Parliament for the City of Oxford, a seat that he
held from 1868 to 1880. His visit coincided with one of the first
entries in Dudley's stud list for his "Special Yellow Retrievers". He
must have been impressed by these dogs, as in years to come, and
a generation later, their offspring would prove to play a very
important part in the development of the breed.

A week may not seem to be long to spend for the shooting at Guisachan, but such excellent sport was to be had on this estate, that it was well worth making a five hundred mile journey…and that was one way! The terrain was very different from his estate at Nuneham Courtney, outside Oxford, which had been in the family for over two hundred years. There was another reason why he did not want to spend more time away from Nuneham. On 31st January 1863, his second child, Lewis Vernon, was born at his London home in Pont Street. Very soon after, his mother, Marie Theresa, nee Lister, died. William's first son, born in 1860, had only lived for eighteen months, and with Lewis showing signs of ill health from birth, he was very concerned for his second son. When it was safe for him to travel, William took his son to the Oxfordshire countryside for the benefit of his health. When he felt that his son had improved sufficiently he made the journey North, just for a week.

William doted on his surviving son and from an early age he called him Loulou. His health continued to give his father cause for concern into his teenage years. One person that shared this concern was William's second wife, Elizabeth Cabot nee Motley, who he married on the 2nd December 1876. Elizabeth was born in Boston, America and she was a widow. Her first husband, Thomas Poynton Ives, had lost his life in the American Civil War. By the time of their marriage, William had a very close relationship with his son. It was so close that Lewis acted as best man at his fathers wedding. Closer still - Lewis went on honeymoon with his father and, by now, his stepmother!

On the 7th May 1878, William and Elizabeth had a son who they named Robert. Bobby, as he was known, and Lewis soon became

Photo 26: Lord Harcourt

happy "brothers", their parents treating them both as equals and despite an age gap of fifteen years they were to remain close throughout their life. In 1881, with the family living at 7 Grafton Street, London, William made Lewis his personal secretary. This role introduced him to the workings of Parliament and within a short time he was mixing with those who held high office, among them the Prime Minister, Mr Gladstone, Dudley Coutts Marjoribanks, and his son Edward. All of those he came in contact with remarked how very different he was from his father. William was known for his blustering and forthright manner, whereas his son was someone who was quickly recognised for his polite manners, his impeccable dress, and his interest in all those that he mixed with. In his early years, Lewis had suffered from lengthy periods of ill health but by the age of eighteen he had developed into a handsome young man. His imposing stature complemented his good looks. He was also very popular with the wives of the MPs, Mrs Gladstone at one time revealing that she had a soft spot for Lewis. Another admirer was Fanny Marjoribanks; and with Elizabeth Harcourt, William's wife, they went with Lewis and Bobby to see the Queen as she was driven through London on the 21st June 1887, to mark Her Majesty's Golden Jubilee. The friendship with the Marjoribanks family was to last for many years. When Edward and Fanny wanted to find out more about their son's teenage crush on Birdie Sutherland, it was to Lewis that they turned to find out "if she was chaste"! After some discreet enquiries, Lewis admitted that he could not find the answer. Within a short time, Edward and Fanny, sent their son to Canada - without Miss Sutherland!

William had looked after the welfare of his son through his early years, caring for him during his frequent bouts of ill health. Their roles were now to be reversed. By the early 1890's it was his father's health that was giving cause for concern and his son took great care to ensure that he provided the fullest support for him to carry out his work in Parliament. On several occasions, William urged his son to stand for a seat in Parliament, but Lewis chose to continue to work alongside his father. He did however support him during the shooting season, and with his stepmother and Bobby they were frequent guests at Guisachan. These were the first times that Lewis saw the Yellow Retrievers. In future years Lewis would play a very important part in the progression of the breed. Both he and his father enjoyed the shooting season, although in his later years his father became more interested in the fishing on the estate.

On the 1st July 1899, Lewis married Mary Ethel Burns at St.Margaret's Church, Westminster. Her parents were both American although she was born in Paris. The wedding was a truly grand occasion with many titled people on the guest list. They spent their honeymoon at Nuneham and it was successful! On the 30th March 1900, their first daughter, Doris Mary Therese was born. Two years later they had another daughter, Olivia Vernon born on the 5th April 1902. Both of these children were born at 14 Berkeley Square, London. During this time, Lewis continued to support his father as his private secretary and he was also taking on more of the day to day running of Nuneham. The Head Gamekeeper at this time was Charles Woodrow, and Ellen, his daughter, was the Kennel Maid. By the early 1900's the kennels had been extended with room for over twenty dogs, and some of these were Yellow Retrievers.

For some time before his marriage, Lewis had taken an increasing interest in the dogs that were being used at Guisachan. He even started to keep a list of the dogs that he had, the first of which was a bitch named Luna, born in 1898 and bred by Lord Tweedmouth. The date given meant that Edward Marjoribanks had bred this dog. The assumption is that it was bred at Guisachan but by this time Yellow Retrievers were also being bred on the Edington Estate and raised by Tom Walker. There is another very interesting entry on this record. The section for "Breed" is entered as, Golden Retriever. This is written by Lewis Harcourt on the list of the dogs that he had and is the first time that I have found this description given for the breed. On the lists that Lord Portsmouth kept, before 1898 he described them as "retriever dogs".

In 1902 the description, Golden Retriever, was acknowledged by the Kennel Club for the breed to be shown as a separate class at Crufts and Championship Shows but it would be another six years before the Golden Retriever was first shown at Crufts.

At the start of 1904, Lewis finally agreed to stand for a seat in Parliament. No doubt his father was delighted! He was elected, unopposed, for the safe Liberal seat of Rossendale, in Lancashire. He took his seat in the House on the 25th March 1904, the same day his father stood down. The House gave their approval on both counts, for Lewis, already well known as his father's private secretary, and for William. Many members expressed their regret that they would no longer witness William's bombastic displays while debating in the House. One would hope that they meant this! Sadly, William did not have a long retirement. A few months later on the 10th October, while at Nuneham he died at the age of 77 following a heart attack. His funeral took place at the New Parish Church at Nuneham, which had been built twenty years previously by his elder brother, Colonel Harcourt. Lewis and his wife lead the

Photo 27: Ellen Woodrow at Lord Harcourt's Kennels 1908

mourners. Among others who attended was the Dowager Lady Tweedmouth, widow of Dudley, the first Lord Tweedmouth, but his son Edward, did not attend. At this time he was still coming to terms with the sad loss of his beloved wife Fanny. William left the estates at Nuneham, and his other estate at Malwood, Hampshire to his son Lewis.

It was at Nuneham that Lewis carried on with the breeding of what must now be classed as the Golden Retriever. On the records that he kept he brought in dogs from a Mr Wareham, a Gamekeeper on the Compton Estate near Sherbourne, Dorset, bred by "L.B. and H.K. Pope" - no records have been found as to where these people came from. In 1905, Lewis also brought in dogs from the 2nd Lord Tweedmouth. For these records he used Nuneham as an affix.

On the 12th February 1908, The Cruft's International Dog Show opened at the Royal Agricultural Hall, Islington, London. The show had been held every year since 1891. The founder of the show was Charles Cruft who was referred to as a "British Showman", although the first shows that he arranged were in France in 1878. At this time Charles was working as a salesman for Spratt's, selling their range of dog biscuits and dog meal. The company still operates today. It brought Charles into contact with a large number of dog breeders and those who were involved in working dogs. His work placed him in an ideal position to let people know of the shows that were planned. Oddly enough it is said that he never had a dog of his own and all attempts to get him to say which breed of dog he would choose if he had one, failed.

Although the Golden Retriever had been recognised for showing as a separate breed since 1902, it was in 1908 that they were first entered at this event. Class 126a in the show catalogue had eight Golden Retrievers listed and they were all owned by The Right Honourable Lewis Harcourt M. P. The breed had made it to the top show in the country. From the few dogs listed by Dudley Coutts Marjoribanks in 1864, they were now being shown at Crufts. They caused quite a sensation, the report from the Grantham Journal of the 15th February summing up what many other newspapers reported: "A golden-haired retriever! Think of it! It is not a stray specimen either. A whole class at Cruft's show in London, on Wednesday, was filled with these "angel dogs". They were entered, too, all in the name of one man, Mr Lewis Harcourt, the genial young statesman. The dogs which form the striking feature of the year's show, are the pick of the Nuneham Kennels". Angel Dogs? Well I suppose they are most of the time! With one person entering the dogs, it is no surprise that one person was awarded first prize - and second and third! Not all of them where bred by Lewis. The first, Brass, was bred by H.K.Pope Esq, second Rossa, by Mr

Wareham. The third place went to, Light, which was bred by Lewis, as was Honey who was reserve. Two other dogs, Crocus and Bracken, were bred by Lewis but not placed, as were Nuneham Sulphur and Nuneham Sol, which had both been bred by the 2nd Lord Tweedmouth in 1905. From this it is more than likely that they were bred at the Edington Estate and had been in the care of Tom Walker. It is interesting that on this occasion, Lewis used Nuneham as the affix for two of the dogs.

The delight people had in seeing the Golden Retievers at Crufts, was repeated later in the year at The Crystal Palace Dog Show. One person who would have been more than pleased to know that they were there was Ishbel, now Lady Aberdeen, who had entered her Skye Terriers. The daughter of Dudley Coutts Marjoribanks, the 1st Lord Tweedmouth, must have been very happy to know that her father's "Special Yellow Retrievers" had made so much progress and were attracting the attention of so many people.

Photo 28: Lord Harcourt's dogs c.1910

Lewis again entered his dogs at Crufts in 1909. By this time he had changed the affix to Culham. He again did well, although he was now in competition with Donald Macdonald. The following year his dog Culham Copper was placed first in the open class. Second place went to Donald Macdonald with Ingestre Scamp. It seems right that Lewis and Donald, who in different ways had done so much for the breed, were rewarded. They came from different positions in life but shared a common interest in the breed that they loved, and were responsible for them coming together at Crufts. The respect that Lewis had for Donald as a breeder was confirmed in 1914 when three dogs, Culham Gem, Culham Tip and Culham Moon, were registered with The Kennel Club and all of them had the Ingestre line in their pedigree.

In 1911, Lewis was again in first place with his dog, Culham Flame, and the following year it was Culham Copper who once again took first place. This was the last year that he entered Crufts but others were to show dogs that were from the Culham line. The classes increased in number, until the outbreak of World War 1, which was to bring a temporary reduction to dog breeding and for a time put a stop to Crufts.

Lewis's wife gave birth to a third daughter on the 28th April 1905. She was named Barbara Vernon. The family was made complete on the 5th October 1908 when Mary gave birth to a son, ensuring that the family line would continue. In remembrance of his father the son was named William.

His father would have been well pleased by the steady progress that his son had made in Parliament. For much of the time he preferred to carry on his work behind the scenes, although he was always well respected. Although he was elected as a Member of Parliament in 1904, it would be another two years before he made his maiden speech, the experience of which he found somewhat daunting. The Prime Minister, Sir Henry Campbell Bannerman, had high regard for him and made him a privy councillor in 1905. He held this post for two years when he was promoted to the cabinet and took on the role of First Commissioner of Works. This gave him the responsibility of looking after all of the parliamentary estate, including parks and palaces. A change of position came in 1910, when the new Prime Minister, Herbert Asquith, appointed him Colonial Secretary. Although it was a surprise to many that he took this appointment, he was again well received by all those he came in contact with. He was to oversee major civil engineering works that took place at this time in Nigeria, which culminated with the completion of a new railway to the main coastal port for the country. In his memory this port was named Port Harcourt.

The work that Lewis had done in Parliament was justifiably recognised by the King in January 1917, when it was agreed that the family viscountcy would be revived, and that Lewis would take the title of Viscount Harcourt. This elevation meant that he could, if he wished, sit in the House of Lords. This he rarely did, preferring to carry on working for the Prime Minister.

The war years took its toll on many politicians. It was difficult for them to cope with the increased amount of work that needed to be attended too. Lewis was spending more time at his London address in Brook Street, Mayfair. The time he was able to spend at Nuneham, was a time that he could relax with his wife and children and his Golden Retrievers, all of which meant so much to him. He also enjoyed seeing the fruition of the plans that he had made for the gardens at Nuneham back in the 1890's. These were admired by all those who visited the estate, as were his dogs.

The strain of the war years eventually started to affect his health. In early 1919 he was diagnosed with heart problems, the symptoms of which were very similar to those that his father had experienced, twenty years previously. With the cessation of war he was able to gradually reduce his workload but he took an active part in the reorganisation of the liberal party, which had been started in 1918. Two years later he began the task of putting his father's papers in order. He enlisted the help of the author and journalist, Alfred Gardner, to get them published. Lewis did not see the result of this as on the morning of the 24th February 1922, his valet found him dead in his bedroom. He had spent the previous evening with Gardner, to discuss the publication of the papers and they had arranged to see each other the following day. A pathologists report, undertaken by Dr. Henry Bright Wier, concluded that the condition of Lewis's heart was more serious than had been diagnosed and the medication that he had been prescribed had unknowingly, had an adverse affect on him. The coroner returned a verdict of death by misadventure. He condemned as utterly grotesque the idea that Lewis had taken his own life. He went on to cite the support that he had given his father when he was alive, and the very valuable work that he had done during his time in Parliament. Setting himself the task of getting his fathers papers into print was not an act of someone contemplating suicide.

Alfred Gardner completed the book in 1923. It provides an insight into the life of William Harcourt and how he was very proud to have a son like Lewis.

After the death of Lewis, his son William succeeded to the title. When he died in 1979, the title came to an end. After Lewis died Mary withdrew from public life. She sold the London home and lived quietly in a small property on the estate at Nuneham. She continued to look after the gardens and for many years had the Golden Retrievers with her, as a loving reminder of her dear husband.

The people who came into contact with Lewis during his time in Parliament all spoke highly of him. He was well respected for his courteous manner and empathy with others. For those who love Golden Retrievers it should always be remembered that Lewis Harcourt was the first person to show them at Cruft's Dog Show and by all accounts they certainly proved that in 1908 they were the talk of the show!

Winifred Maude Charlesworth (nee Fleming)

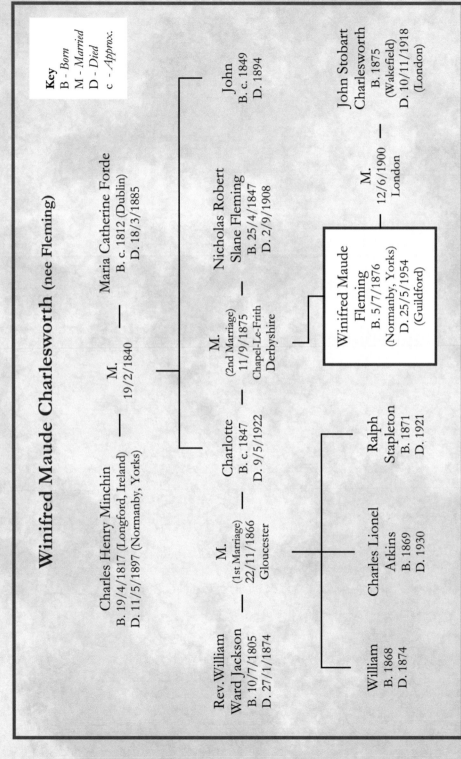

Key
B - *Born*
M - *Married*
D - *Died*
c - *Approx.*

Charles Henry Minchin
B. 19/4/1817 (Longford, Ireland)
D. 11/5/1897 (Normanby, Yorks)

M.
19/2/1840

Maria Catherine Forde
B. c. 1812 (Dublin)
D. 18/3/1885

John
B. c. 1849
D. 1894

Nicholas Robert
Slane Fleming
B. 25/4/1847
D. 2/9/1908

M.
(2nd Marriage)
11/9/1875
Chapel-Le-Frith
Derbyshire

Charlotte
B. c. 1847
D. 9/5/1922

Rev. William
Ward Jackson
B. 10/7/1805
D. 27/1/1874

M.
(1st Marriage)
22/11/1866
Gloucester

Ralph
Stapleton
B. 1871
D. 1921

Charles Lionel
Atkins
B. 1869
D. 1930

William
B. 1868
D. 1874

Winifred Maude
Fleming
B. 5/7/1876
(Normanby, Yorks)
D. 25/5/1954
(Guildford)

M.
12/6/1900
London

John Stobart
Charlesworth
B. 1875
(Wakefield)
D. 10/11/1918
(London)

❧ 7 ❧

Mrs. Winifred Maude Charlesworth

(5th July 1876 - 25th May 1954)

Foundations for the Future

T HE FIRST YELLOW RETRIEVER recorded by Dudley Coutts
Marjoribanks in his stud book was Nous, who was listed in
1865. At this time he was a year old. The photo of Nous with the
Gamekeepers at Guisachan taken about 1870, shows him in a pose
that indicates he is fully trained for the work that was expected of
him. By the early 1900's the breed, now known as the Golden
Retriever, had been accepted as a welcome addition to the various
types of gundogs, who with others in this class of dog, all had their
own merits. The Goldens also had their critics, some of whom cited
their lack of uniformity and poor work rate. This did not hinder the
breed being accepted by a large number of people, attracted by their
gentle nature, always dependable and willing to please. It meant that
they were to be found in places away from the highlands of
Scotland. They found favour in Southern England and the large
estates in Staffordshire and in the South West of Ireland. Added to
this they were seen at dog shows. The first of these had been local
events - you know the type, waggiest tail, lovable eyes, the dog the
judge would most like to take home - how many Goldens won this
class? By the early 1900's the railways had expanded to such an

extent that it meant that travelling greater distances to attend shows had become easier. As the railway network grew the type and content of shows also changed. There were shows which had classes for separate breeds, as well as open and Championship shows, the Gamekeeper Show and Crufts, where the Goldens first appeared in 1908. Added to this were the shows that were arranged around the country by the growing number of breed clubs, many of which still survive today. The value of these clubs was that people from around the country could come together and share their experience of the breed and to gain knowledge that would benefit their development. At the start of the 1900's the Golden Retriever had not gained sufficient popularity to support its own breed club. This was soon to change with the very redoubtable determination of Mrs W. M. Charlesworth. For over forty years she was a true champion of the breed supporting them on the show bench and using them in field trials.

Winifred Maude Charlesworth nee Fleming, was born on the 5th July 1876 at Normanby Hall, Yorkshire. Her mother, Charlotte nee Minchin, was born in Dublin in 1847. By 1866 Charlotte had come to England and was living with her father, Charles Henry Minchin, in the Old Trafford district of Manchester. Charlotte's first marriage was to the Reverend William Ward Jackson. It took place on the 22nd November 1866 at the Church of St Mary de Lode, in the grounds of Gloucester Cathedral. At this time, William was the owner of Normanby Hall, a property that had been in the family since 1748. The wedding was a real family affair, and no doubt a celebration of William, then aged 61, taking a bride of 19. The service was conducted by the Reverend Henry Minchin, cousin of the bride, and he was assisted by, Thomas Sanctuary, the Venerable Archdeacon of Dorset, Nephew of the bridegroom. Within five

Photo 29: Mrs. Charlesworth in
Women's Voluntary Reserve uniform

years they had three sons, William, born in 1868, Charles Lionel, 1869 and Ralph Stapleton, 1871. Charlotte's joy in her young family was brought to an abrupt end on the 27th January 1874, when her husband died at the age of 69. By the end of this year she also lost her eldest son, William. A dear husband and son, both named William, passing away within a year.

The sadness that had come into Charlotte's life did not put her off marriage and a year later, on the 11th September 1875 she married Nicholas Slane Fleming, at Chapel-en-le-Frith, Derbyshire. Nicholas was the same age as Charlotte and on his wedding certificate his occupation was given as shipping agent. Despite the fact that the marriage took place in Derbyshire within a short space of time they had moved back Normanby Hall where they were to live all their married life. On the 5th July 1876 Charlotte gave birth to a daughter, who was christened Winifred Maude.

Winifred may well have been the daughter that Charlotte had longed for. Charlotte kept the family unit around her, and it is evident that they were all treated equally. The 1881census for Normanby Hall shows Charlotte with her husband Nicholas, as head of the household, their youngest stepson, Ralph Ward Jackson, their daughter, Winifred, the unmarried sisters of Nicholas, Annie and Charlotte, and Charlotte's brother, John with his wife Emily and their son Lionel. Added to this there where eight household staff to look after them. Ten years later six family members are listed and there were thirteen household staff. Once again the family appear to have come together for the census with Charlotte and her husband Nicholas, Charlotte's father Charles Minchin and their daughter Winifred, now 14 years old. Also listed are her half brothers, Charles Lionel and Ralph Stapleton. The census provides the information that both of these had no occupation and were living on their own means. Charles Lionel, the eldest, at 22, was by now the head of the household. He had acquired this position, on his 21st birthday on the 31st January 1890. Prior to this the Hall and the estates had been held in trust after his fathers death in 1874.

There is no evidence that Winifred attended an official school. It is more than likely that she and her half-brothers were educated at the Hall with the census for 1881 and 1891 listing a school governess. When they came of age, both Charles Lionel and Ralph Stapleton went to Eton to finish their schooling. There were plenty of outside activities for Winifred to be involved in. The estate extended to over 1,700 acres, with some parts let out to tenant farmers, which still left ample land for Winifred's father to undertake the breeding of horses, which were always needed at this time to assist with work on the estate and the surrounding farms. By 1885 her father had extended his horse breeding activities away from Yorkshire and he became a member of the Hackney Stud Book Society which co-operated with the Shire Horse Society to stage horse shows at various venues around the country. At this early age, Winifred was taking an interest in the breeding of the horses and the shows that her father was attending. It was not long before Winifred was up on a horse and soon became an accomplished horsewoman. By her late teenage years she accompanied her father on his visits to shows, not all of which where confined to horses. It was in 1895 that with both her mother and father, she attended the Cleveland Hunt Puppy Show at Skelton-in-Cleveland held in association with the Hunt Show. One would like to think that this show had a marked effect on the young Winifred. There were not only classes for horses but also for dogs with the emphasis on puppies. After the judging, the family were amongst the invited guests for lunch, laid out in a large marquee on the lawns of Skelton Castle.

Winifred may not have had the schooling that would have benefited her half brothers, but her father was increasingly involving her in local community events to bring her into contact with people of high regard in the locality. No doubt he had it in mind that she should be given the opportunity to meet suitable men with the possibility of a future union and to this end he enlisted the assistance of her half brother, Charles Lionel Ward Jackson. By the 1890's Charles was in the Yorkshire Hussars. He had been promoted to the position of Captain and Honorary Major by 1893, and a year later he was on the guest list at the Yorkshire Hussars Centenary Ball, held in York on the 5th December 1894. Also on the guest list were Mr and Mrs Fleming and Miss Fleming. The event was described as "a brilliant spectacle" well attended by Lords and Ladies and their siblings, the latter no doubt also looking for a partner in life. There were several members of the church. A midweek event was good for them, the next day they could sleep off their hangover, and of course many members of the military all regaled in their uniform. What effect did this all have on the 18-year-old Miss Fleming? That we cannot tell but six years later she did marry a soldier although he was not on the guest list at this ball.

During the 1890's Winifred's father was to rely more and more on his daughter to arrange the Normanby Show, held in the grounds of the Hall every August. The display and judging of the horses still came first but there was increasing interest being given to the showing of dogs. Seeing what Winifred was to achieve in future years it is more than likely that she was developing an outlook that everything is possible if one puts ones mind to it. Any problem that came her way in the arranging of these shows she made sure were solved well in time to make the occasion a success. Her skill and enthusiasm was remarked on when she arranged a fancy dress ball to raise funds for a new organ for Christ Church, the Parish Church at Eston near Normanby. For many years her father had got her

Photo 30: Mrs. Charlesworth

involved. This time the roles were reversed with Winifred getting her father to be one of the Master's of Ceremonies. This event took place on the 5th April 1899. It was very successful but it was to be the last event she arranged in this area. Within six months she was living in London.

In October 1899, a notification was given at the church of St. Paul's, Knightsbridge that a marriage had been arranged between John Stobart, eldest son of Mr. C.E.Charlesworth of Owston Hall, Doncaster, and Winifred Maude, only child of Mr. N.R.Fleming of Crossbeck House, Normanby, Middlesborough. Where they met is not known but John Stobart Charlesworth was a 2nd Lieutenant in the Yorkshire Dragoons so he could have been introduced to her by one of her half brothers at one of the balls that were held at or near Normanby. There is no explanation as to why she was living in London at 22, Park Lane, Mayfair, at the end of 1899. This is the first of a number of mysteries, which appeared to surround her later life. It could be the way she wanted it. By this time she had some distinct militant tendencies, which were shown in the lack of true information she was prepared to reveal to the official authorities. Whatever the reason they were married on the 12th June 1900. From now on despite what the future may have in store for her, to the dog world she was always known and respected as Mrs Charlesworth.

It has often been said that the marriage only lasted seven days. This is not supported by the 1901 census although it has to be pointed out that there were three different versions of where they were and if one follows the theory of her being reluctant to reveal to the authorities their location, by now her husband was just as culpable of going along with her reluctance to give information.

So, for the 1901 census it's a case of take your pick with regard to Winifred and John. Either living at Monk Fryston, Yorkshire, John Charlesworth, age 25, married, born Wakefield, Winifred Maude Charlesworth, age 24, wife, born Normanby, or living at Crossbeck House, Eston, Yorkshire. Winifred Maude Charlesworth, age 23, married, born Normanby, or for her husband at Harrow Road, Aldershot, John Stobart Charlesworth, age 25, married, born Wakefield. This last address was the barracks, where if this census is correct, John was stationed with his regiment, the Yorkshire Dragoons. If the information on the first of these is correct then they were together for much longer than a week. The 1911 census does not help as neither of them are on it. Was this another example of them turning their back on the authorities? Did they prefer to give them a two fingered salute? At some time they did go their own ways, but for what reason? Was he a philanderer? Did one of them not relish the physical contact of marriage? For whatever reason Winifred did not revert back to her maiden name and was always known by those in the sporting and canine world as Mrs Charlesworth.

I have suggested that John and Winifred could have met one another through an introduction by her half brother, Charles Lionel Atkins Ward Jackson at one of the regimental balls, as he and John were both in the Army. Another possibility could be on the sporting field. John was a keen huntsman with the York and Ainsty and Bramham Hunts and Winifred, before she moved to London, was taking an increased interest in dogs and their breeding. Her enthusiasm to breed dogs meant that she had new kennels built adjacent to Crossbeck House, which was in the grounds of the Normanby Estate. In 1908 she had applied for and obtained the affix, Holyport, and used this to register two Cocker Spaniels in that year. Her involvement with Cockers did not last long as she soon turned her interest to the retriever. In a book that she wrote in 1935 she stated that she obtained her first retriever "on the advice of a Parson Upcher", although she gives no details as to where they were when she was given this advice. The Upcher family came from Norfolk, where several generations of the family entered the ministry. There were so many of them with "Reverend" before their name that you can imagine the problems that arose when they had to agree who would offer up thanks for, no doubt, the very fine food that had been prepared for them at the frequent family gatherings. Fine food it must have been, when it is known that a lot of them took a serious interest in field sports of all kinds, so there was always a plentiful supply of game. A Parson Upcher may have given her advice on what breed of dog to have - she may even have seen a retriever being worked - but she does not say she got one of these dogs from him or anyone else in the Upcher family.

Mrs Charlesworth must have been impressed by what the parson had told her about the breed as by 1908 she had got a bitch. This was registered in 1912 with the name of Normanby Beauty. It was born on the 1st June 1906, but there is no mention of the breeder or who the sire or dam was but by September 1908 she had used Beauty for her first litter. For this she used one of the best dogs at the time for the mating, with Lord Harcourt's dog, Culham Brass being the sire. From this litter, two dogs, Normanby Bruce and Normanby Buck were registered in June 1911 to a Mr and Mrs Bennett. A third dog, was kept by Mrs Charlesworth. When she registered this dog in November 1909 for some reason she used the Holyport affix, naming the dog, Holyport Buck and recording that the dam was Holyport Beauty. On the registration of the dogs that were with Mr and Mrs Bennett the other two dogs from the litter, the dam was recorded as Normanby Beauty!

What did Mrs Charlesworth mean by all this? Did she set out to confuse people by using the Holyport affix? Or was it a slip of the pen?

Again she may have given incorrect information, when she came to have her first dog. In an article in the Illustrated Kennel News for the 12th December 1913, she stated that she purchased her first retriever dog from "a keeper in Scotland". This dog was registered with the Kennel Club, as Normanby Tweedledum with the sire being a dog by the name of Sandy of Wavertree and the dam being a bitch by the name of Yellow Nell. The breeder is listed as "unknown". However, on the 9th October 1909, Yellow Nell was registered, being in the ownership of a John Hindmarsh. He was born in Northumberland, and both the sire and the dam were out of the Ingestre line and were kept by Donald Macdonald. At this time John Hindmarsh was the Gamekeeper on the Sandon Park estate owned by the Earl of Harrowby. This estate was next to Ingestre. Was the report "a keeper in Scotland" incorrect? Should the report have stated "a keeper from Scotland"?

Whatever the truth of Mrs Charlesworth's first retriever and her registration - and it is very difficult to get the truth after so many years, it was to be the start of one persons determination to popularise the breed over the next forty years both in working tests and in the show ring. Within a few years her line was to be found winning prizes around the country. Along the way she did encounter some problems both in show and field trial events. It was at Crufts in 1913 that her name first appeared exhibiting Noraby

Beauty! Noraby? Did she make this mistake on her entry form or was it the fault of the Kennel Club? Who ever it was Mrs Charlesworth was disqualified. A few months after this, she changed her affix for all future registrations to "Normanby". Whoever made the mistake one would hope that Mrs Charlesworth kept it in mind that a year previously one of her dogs, Normanby Bruce had been shown by a Mr and Mrs Bennett.

At field trials she also had some problems but on one notable occasion it was herself who was responsible. At the Irish Field Trials on the 6th December 1913, she worked Normanby Tweedledum. The dog had worked all day and was well placed to obtain a Certificate of Merit. At the end of the dogs final test, Mrs Charlesworth was talking to a friend, possibly giving her some advice, and forgot to put Tweedledum on the lead. Suddenly a shot rang out and a duck dropped into the nearby lake. Tweedledum did not need any command - he was off! The temptation was too great. He wanted to prove he was a retriever! Mrs Charlesworth and Tweedledum were immediately disqualified. Had she been telling her friend how important it was to get your dog on the lead once its test was over? How many times have I been told to do this? If only the dogs would not wriggle so much!

Mrs Charlesworth travelled many miles around the country showing her dogs as far apart as Edinburgh, Manchester and London. In early 1915 she also agreed to undertake one of her few judging appointments travelling to Birmingham for their annual show. Like others she often used the railway to travel to the shows. Her attendance at these events never took precedence over working her dogs. She was a great believer in ensuring that any of the breed that

Photo 31: Mrs. Charlesworth
Surrey & West Sussex Trials, 1926

sat on the show bench should be capable of working a full day in the field, something that she did for many years.

Although her visits to the kennels at Crossbeck House were at times limited, she did not forget her family. In 1912 she lent Normanby Sandy to her half brother, Capt. Charles Lionel Ward-Jackson, who at this time was living at Shobden Court, Herefordshire. He worked the dog on his grounds during the winter. This provided Charles with a dog that was already trained to the gun and provided the breed with some exposure in an area where up until this time they had been rarely seen. No doubt Mrs Charlesworth benefited from the exposure as well. Her time was also taken up in robustly defending the breed whenever she felt that criticism of them was unjust. She did this through the printed media of the time. She wrote many letters to The Field, The Shooting Times, The Kennel Gazette and Our Dogs. These letters often provided some quite amusing replies defending the breed. When someone expressed their view that London was not the place to keep and exercise a dog, her pen was quickly put to paper and she wrote that she had no problem with keeping her dogs in London or in giving them exercise. Everyday, when she was in the capital, she gave her chauffeur instructions to drop her and the dogs on the north side of Hyde Park and collect them on the south side in one hour and thirty minutes - precisely! However, it must be said of her, she was always willing to give assistance and advice to anyone that was starting with the breed. There was one condition. Do not ask for her assistance and help if you do not like what she would tell you!

In 1913, Mrs Charlesworth decided to form a club that would work solely for the interest of the breed, to promote its health and welfare in both show and field trials, and to introduce a standard of points for the breed. The standards would act as a guideline for judges to assess the quality of the dogs being shown. This club was to be known as the Golden Retriever Club. The club still exists to this day. By August of 1913 voting had taken place and those elected were given in the publication Our Dogs on the 29th August 1913. The following people were elected.

Presidents
Mrs Charlesworth, Lieut. Col. Hendley,
F.W.Herbert, Mr.G.H.K.Bone

Vice Presidents
E.King, F.W.Morris, Capt.Fraser Newall, A.Randolph

Committee
Lieut-Col Hendley, Capt. Loftus, Miss Crawshay,
F.W.Morris, F.W.Herbert, D.Macdonald, G.King,
A Wallace, Mr G.H.K.Bone

Quite a lot of people for a fledgling club, but it does show that by this time there was a good mix of people who either wanted to show or to work them. Among the latter was Donald Macdonald, who had shown dogs longer than anyone else. He had been in the show ring with Lord Harcourt and Mrs Charlesworth and he had bought and used dogs from others for mating, and for the purpose of working and showing them. More people were added to the committee at the annual meeting in February 1914. It was at this meeting that the first set of accounts were passed showing a balance of £5 12s 9d. Also agreed on at this meeting was that special prizes were to be given for puppies entered at championship shows and that the selection of judges at these shows, would be decided upon by the secretary, - who was? You have guessed correctly! - Mrs Charlesworth!

Within six months of the meeting of the Golden Retriever Club held in 1914, the country was at war. At first, most things continued as they were, with shows and working events taking place almost as normal. It soon became apparent that the war would go on for longer than was expected and in late 1914 Mrs Charlesworth joined the Women's Volunteer Reserve. This had been formed by Lady Londonderry   and the Hon. Evelina Haresfield and the object was to support the war effort by recruiting women who would be willing to be trained in First Aid, signalling, driving vehicles, camp cooking, handicraft and fencing. Women already trained for these disciplines were more than welcome and one discipline which was added to this was rifle shooting, in which Mrs Charlesworth was more than competent. This valuable attribute assisted her to be made commanding officer, working by June 1915 at the Baker Street offices of the WVR. This was convenient for The Haven, in Cromwell Mews, West London, where she was now living. The property was large enough to have five of her Golden Retrievers with her, all of whom went to the office with her taken by car, driven by the chauffeur! It was not only at Baker Street that she worked. She often put in long days at the canteen in Woolwich. None of this prevented her from attending dog shows that were in the locality. One of these was the Ladies Kennel Association show in London in July of that year. On this occasion it was reported that she was congratulated on attending the show in her khaki uniform, issued to women working for the WVR, the reason being that she had no time to return home to change and did not want to disappoint the dogs. When she moved to London she also brought her rifle, which she used on Sundays, her one day off during the week. On this day she took the dogs to Berkshire for them to work. The war was not going to stop her from enjoying the company of her dogs or to able to work them.

Not all the original members of the Golden Retriever Club could carry on with their committee duties or in some cases continue to have their dogs. Donald Macdonald was ordered to spend more time at Ingestre to cover the reduced number of Gamekeepers on the estate, due to them enlisting, but he did keep his dogs. Capt. Hendley, from Pitfar in Perthshire had to disperse his kennel after he was called back to military duty at Woolwich. Rhona Crawshay sold all of her Goldens, although it took a long time to find a buyer, and she also joined the WVR working on the clothes collection service for injured soldiers. Mrs Ames, a late appointment to the original committee, moved to Southern Ireland where her husband's regiment had been moved and where he was to work as the adjutant at the barracks. She took the dogs with her and was not affected by the threat of restrictions on breeding of dogs and was successful with more than one litter.

Photo 32: The Ladies Kennel Association
Regents Park, London, 1913

As the war went on there were less dog shows although Crufts did continue until 1916 but the entries were much reduced. Donald Macdonald, Mrs Ames and Mrs Charlesworth all showed dogs at this event. There were few field trials by this time. The reduced number of Gamekeepers on the estates meant that the results from breeding the game birds were poor. With the large number of men enlisting there were not the volunteer beaters available to organise a good days shoot.

When the war finally ended, the Golden Retriever, like many breeds had survived. The Golden Retriever Club still existed. Credit for this was very much down to Mrs Charlesworth who by the end of the war had given service to the country and who had remained loyal to the breed that gave her and others so much pleasure.

The remainder of the life of Mrs Charlesworth is outside of the years for which this book has been written. However a few items need to be recorded.

She died on the 25th May 1954 at the Royal Surrey County Hospital in Guildford, from a Coronary Thrombosis. She was cremated at Woking on 30th May 1954. Her will, dated January 1953, stated that there were to be no flowers, no mourning and that her two remaining dogs should be "painlessly destroyed". She makes no mention of the breed of dog.

Her "husband", John Stobart Charlesworth died 10th November 1918. He died from Pneumonia. He was buried at Knaresborough Cemetery. He appointed his brother, William Grice Charlesworth as his executor. There was no mention in his will of his "wife" Winifred Maude Charlesworth.

From 1920 to 1954 Mrs Charlesworth lived at fourteen different addresses in the South of England. During this time there is no evidence that she lived at Normanby Hall. Today the property stands as a semi-derelict ruin.

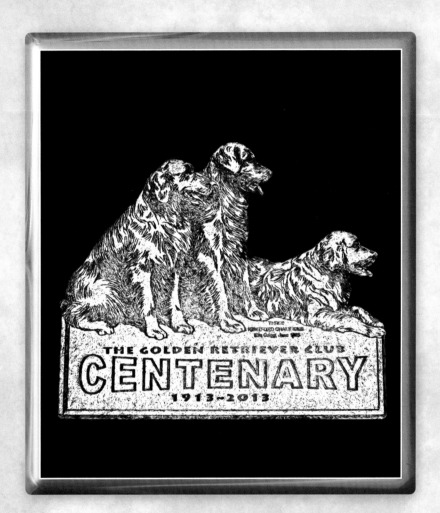

～ 8 ～

Tailpiece

T HE LIVES OF the people I have written about in these seven chapters varied greatly but they all shared an interest in dogs and enjoyed an outdoor lifestyle that meant that they had a full knowledge of the countryside.

Among these people are those who attained their wealth from financial institutions and directorships of large companies. Politicians, whose family represented a constituency from one generation to another. There are those who worked on the land, with their daily tasks being dictated by the elements and the seasons of the year. Added to this was a person who was able to live off her own means and could have pleased herself what she did, but instead became very influential in the progress of the breed. Some worked alongside others and despite their different status in life it was never a hindrance to forming a mutual understanding and respect for each other that meant that they often worked together for many years. They had the satisfaction of service well given on both sides. What brought them all together was the development of the Golden Retriever.

The individual contributions to the development of the dogs were varied but they were all related, each of them adding to the progress of the breed. It was Dudley Coutts Marjoribanks who kept a list of all of his dogs for over forty years at his kennels at Guisachan. This included all the breeds that he had. When he listed the Retrievers you get a sense that he took greater care and included more details, where they came from and who looked after them on the estate. This information supports his daughter, Ishbel, who often said they were his "Special Yellow Retrievers". His son Edward also recognised this, and when he brought his dear wife, Fanny, to Guisachan, these dogs very quickly had a new companion to share the long days working in the hills. Lord and Lady Tweedmouth and the Marjoribanks family, shared their lives with the estate workers, willingly giving their support to make their own lives as comfortable as possible. Many of them were in service to them for many years and had great respect for them. Duncan MacLennan, who became Head Stalker, worked on the estate for over fifty years. At the Edington Estate in Berwickshire, also owned by the Marjoribanks family, the head Gamekeeper, Tom Walker, worked the retrievers for 36 years. During all of this time the retrievers were being recognised more and more. Further progress for the breed came from another Scotsman, Donald Macdonald, who was at the Earl of Shrewsbury's estate at Ingestre, Staffordshire, for 32 years. He showed the dogs for the first time at the Gamekeepers Dog Show at Shrewsbury in 1912. His success here, and at others shows meant that his dogs were used by other breeders, again adding to their increasing popularity. By now it was not just the Gamekeepers who recognised the benefits of the breed. The gentry also continued to have a strong liking for them and it was Lord Harcourt who gave them the title of Golden Retriever, showing them at Crufts for the first time in 1908 when they made such a great impression. Then there was Mrs Charlesworth. She promoted the breed for over forty years and insisted that while the breed graced the show bench they should not only be fit for showing but also fit enough to do a full days work. Although she was sometimes controversial in her opinions, on this point she was correct. With their long association with the breed, all of these people left a very valuable legacy.

In the 1920's, when Mrs Charlesworth made the comment about the fitness of the breed and her valid opinion that the dogs should be worked, the country had a far different aspect to it than it has now in the early 21st century. After two world wars large shooting estates had either to be sold off or to be radically reduced in size. This in turn meant that the number of people employed for a good days shoot, involving retrievers of all breeds has been reduced. However, the Golden Retriever is still very popular with over 7,000 being registered with the Kennel Club in 2013. They are still worked - Mrs Charlesworth would be delighted! - they make an ideal family pet - Mrs Charlesworth would not be quite so delighted - and most of the pets are well behaved - Mrs Charlesworth's comments? So they should be - if not train them properly!

With restrictions in some areas where they can be used for the purpose of what they were bred for, they have proved to be very adaptable. They are still seen in large numbers of dog shows, some of which are solely for the breed. They are trained to take part in agility and obedience competitions and compare very favourably with other breeds. To see sixteen Golden Retrievers working with their handlers, for heelwork in different formations all set to music, as in the Southern Golden Retriever Display Team, has given enjoyment and pleasure to thousands of people at events, from village fetes to Discover Dogs and Crufts. These events help to bring the breed to the notice of the public and sustain their popularity.

They can provide loyalty and support to those who are disabled in life. Given the right training, they respond to being an ideal Guide Dog for those who have lost their sight. They are also trained as PATdogs, allowing them to enter Residential Homes, to act as therapy to those who need to be nursed and in doing so they often bring back happy memories for those in care.

Medical Detection Dogs also trains them to help people with life-threatening health conditions. These dogs give their 'owners' confidence, a better quality of life, greater independence and above all save their lives on a daily basis.

The breed has evolved and changed for over 150 years. It has taken on new roles and fulfilled them to the great satisfaction of many people. The breed will no doubt continue to evolve, but all those who truly love the Golden Retriever should ensure that they always keep their loving and gentle nature.

Despite all the new disciplines that they are now trained for, there is no better sight than seeing them sent to retrieve game. That's what they were bred for. Let's hope it continues for many years to come.

THE TALE KEEPS WAGGING…

Hidden away in archives throughout the country there is no doubt more to be found about what we now know as the Golden Retriever and the people who first brought them into the canine world. There are other theories and opinions as to how this happened and some people believe these to this day. In a lot of the records a circus often comes into the story.

During the writing of this book, I found a snippet of information, which does appear to be rather curious. Dudley Coutts Marjoribanks, the 1st Lord Tweedmouth, bought a ranch in America for his sons, Coutts and Archie, for them to breed cattle. During the time they were there, a number of retrievers were sent to them, to keep them company and remind them of home. Within two years of their father's death the value of shares in the Meux's Brewery, which had been left to the two sons, had halved. Archie's health was also giving cause for concern and in 1898 he sold his half of the ranch to his brother and returned to England. With him was his American wife, Elizabeth Trimble nee Brown, and they went to live at Prior Park, Bath, near to where Archie's mother, the Dowager Lady Tweedmouth lived. In 1900 Archie died, and his wife, Elizabeth, who was also known as "Mysie" Brown, went to live with Lady Tweedmouth as her companion at her home in Bath. Also with them were the retrievers that had come back from America.

In 1905 the Dowager sold her last property in Scotland, Kerrow House on the Guisachan estate and moved to London to be with her eldest son Edward. The retrievers also had to move. They went to Edington, - "Granny" said so - to be with Tom Walker and Duncan McGillivray. They all went back to Scotland - from The Circus! This was the address where the Dowager had lived in Bath! By the way it was number 5!!

With a wag of the tale we are now at the end of this trail - for the time being!